Understanding Society through Popular Music

The purpose of this book is to use music as a tool to help students understand the structure and process of social life. Sociologically, music is important because it simultaneously contains and reflects a people's language, values, feelings, concerns, and goals. The material in this innovative, compact supplement is current and relevant to the musical experiences of today's college and university students and includes a companion website that features an instructor's guide, test bank, discussion questions, and links to relevant internet sites. To make the book easy to use in introductory sociology courses, it is structured along lines parallel to the way most instructors teach the course.

Joseph A. Kotarba is Professor of Sociology at the University of Houston and is author of several books including a forthcoming work on baby boomers and rock and roll fans. His musical tastes range from Henry Purcell to Van Morrison.

Phillip Vannini is Assistant Professor in the School of Communication and Culture at Royal Roads University. He is editor of *Body/ Embodiment* and *Material Culture and Technology in Everyday Life*. His musical faith rests in the power of progressive hardcore and in the soothing melody of space and symphony rock.

Understanding Society through Popular Music

Joseph A. Kotarba and
Phillip Vannini

Routledge
Taylor & Francis Group

NEW YORK AND LONDON

First published 2009
by Routledge
270 Madison Ave, New York, NY 10016

Simultaneously published in the UK
by Routledge
2 Park Square, Milton Park, Abingdon, Oxon OX14 4RN

Routledge is an imprint of the Taylor & Francis Group, an informa business

© 2009 Taylor & Francis

Typeset in Minion by
RefineCatch Limited, Bungay, Suffolk
Printed and bound in the United States of America on acid-free paper by
Edwards Brothers, Inc.

Library of Congress Cataloging in Publication Data
Kotarba, Joseph.
  Understanding society through popular music / Joseph Kotarba, Phillip Vannini.
    p. cm.
  Includes bibliographical references
1. Popular music–Social aspects–United States.   I. Vannini, Phillip.   II. Title.
  ML3918.P67K67 2009
  306.4′8424–dc22

                                                                    2007053033

ISBN10: 0–415–95408–8 (hbk)
ISBN10: 0–415–95409–6 (pbk)
ISBN10: 0–203–89460–X (ebk)

ISBN13: 978–0–415–95408–2 (hbk)
ISBN13: 978–0–415–95409–9 (pbk)
ISBN13: 978–0–203–89460–6 (ebk)

Visit the companion website: www.routledge.com/textbooks/9780415954099

CONTENTS

PREFACE

Is music playing in the background as you are reading this? If not, you might consider turning it on. After all, music was almost always on when we were writing this book. Old school rock and heavy metal, indie rock, ambient, classical, folk; whatever we were in the mood for. Sometimes we weren't in the mood for anything but the people around us seemed to be. So we listened (we had to) to cartoon songs, to fleeting bits of rap as tricked-up base-cars zoomed by our offices, or to the next door neighbor blaring Bocelli's opera through the open windows on a warm summer day. Perhaps, as we were thinking about re-organizing our table of contents, we hummed the song you just cannot get out of your mind, as George did with the Broadway musical on the classic *Seinfeld* episode. Whatever it was, whenever it was, wherever it was, music was on for us, and unless it really distracts you from reading you might want to turn it on now too. It will complement the reading experience. Trust us: after all we're experts, aren't we?

There. Now that it's on nice and loud or maybe just as background noise, let's discuss what we are doing here. Many people from different backgrounds—or from different "socio-economic-cultural backgrounds" as we say in sociology—commonly experience music as the soundtrack of their everyday lives. Indeed, it seems as if a tune is always accompanying our daily rhythms: from the wake-up call through our alarm radio and our favorite morning tunes on the ride to work and school, to the beats of campus life or office cubicle culture, and from the gas pumps to the supermarket and health club. Not to mention music television, ubiquitous MP3 players and Discmans, movie scores, and the very sounds and melodies of the spaces that surround us: from the chirping of sparrows to the crashing of waves. Music is everywhere. Even Phillip's roofers, currently working above his head, seem more preoccupied with their music than the warning sounds of thunder and the coming storm (or the loud sound of their own hammering). There is a sonorous dimension for everything: for every purpose, every group of listeners, every mood, and every occasion. And everywhere we listen, music comes to us (or from us) as a product: the product of technological relations which resulted in its creation and distribution; the product of geographic dimensions which shape trends, availability, and connection to space and place; the product of historical periods which shape fashions, costs, expectations, and considerations on what is appropriate or not appropriate; the product of social classes, genders, age-groups, and ethnicities, each with their relation to preferred forms of musical styles; as well as the product of familial, religious, and biographic particulars which influence the tunes that strike a chord with our heart and our sense of self. Indeed, ask yourself what you did when we asked you to turn some music on: did you look for your MP3 library? Scrambled to dig out your latest favorite CD? Rolled the dial to find your favorite radio station? Turn on MTV? Whatever you did, and whatever we all do, music is not just the product of harmony, melody, and rhythm relations, but perhaps more importantly a *social* product. Many people are involved with creation of our musical experiences, as well as our music *per se*.

As a social product, music is a prime object of sociological investigation. Sociology examines both the processes and outcomes through which diverse forms of sociality take place. In light of that, studying a song or musical preferences is no different from studying a form of collective organization or the particular shape that labor relations take in a country. If sociology is the study of what people do together, and if music is something that people do together, then the sociological study of music is as "natural" as the sociological study of class, gender, race, social organization, or identity. In spite of this, the sociological study of popular music has not always been as common as the sociological examination of, say, the economy. Sociologists in the past have often felt that music and all forms of popular culture were too trivial for serious social scientific business. Thus, at best, music was treated as a derivative of basic social structures, pegged as an opiate of the masses, and scoffed at (under the guise of theory) for being less refined than it should have been. But, as we are going to discuss in our Introduction, things have changed. After the advent of the so-called "cultural turn" in social sciences—itself a symptom of the great cultural shifts shaping most of Western society in the 1960s and early 1970s—sociologists and other cultural science scholars began to closely heed the advice of those like the critical theorists of the Frankfurt School and the urban ethnographers of the Chicago School, who were pushing for a wider definition of culture as a broad way of life. As those movements unfolded, popular music and popular culture in general began to occupy a more central role in sociological endeavors.

The study of popular music has now evolved into a substantial area of interest among many English-speaking sociologists in the past twenty-five years. Sociologists in the United States and Canada—as well as in other countries, especially Great Britain—have witnessed the growth of popular music as both a societal as well as cultural force. In doing so they have begun to reflect on the links between musical production, distribution, and consumption, and the behaviors, emotions, and thoughts of music fans, the intentions of producers and distributers, the consequences on local and global cultures and social organization and more. Thus, just as it is typical for sociology in general, we have scholars of popular music who focus on the economy of music, or on the social regulation and organization of music-making, on the technology and culture of sound, on the relation between identity, gender, and music, and so forth. In writing this book we hope to survey the vast diversity of popular music studies and the vast diversity of sociological study. Of course, we can only aim to skim, at best, this great body of knowledge, but in doing so we hope to introduce you to an exciting body of sociological knowledge hopefully of interest to you.

In fact, the aim of this textbook is to integrate growing interest in the sociological study of popular music with mainstream sociological instruction. Our book has a take on popular music that reflects, while taking advantage of, the growing sophistication of the field. In writing it, we benefit from the work of several researchers of popular music who have laid out the terrain before us. The seminal early textbook on the sociology of popular music, Simon Frith's famous *Sound Effects* (1981) has been a mainstay in numerous courses over the past seventeen years. Frith focuses on a range of topics central to the world of popular music itself: the history of rock 'n' roll; the roots of rock 'n' roll in country music and the blues; popular music and politics; the popular music industry; and so forth. More recent texts that have left a mark on this territory include Andy Bennett's *Cultures of Popular Music* (2001) and Reebee Garofalo's *Rockin' Out* (2007). These fine texts illustrate two major themes in the ways the sociology of popular music is organized. The former, on the one hand, emphasizes the great varieties of styles of popular music as well as the lifestyles and subcultures that give life to these musical styles. In such text we learn about the social and cultural particulars underlying surf, punk, heavy metal, and other styles of music. The latter, on the other hand, emphasizes the chronology of historical events that have shaped popular music: early rock-a-billy; the advent of mechanical reproduction of music; the Civil Rights movement and the war in Vietnam; the end of the Cold War; the corporatization of music; and the current era of pop and rap. Numerous other texts which you can access to advance your understanding of the social and cultural dynamics of popular music—as we ourselves have done—exist. *Popular Music Studies* by David Hesmondhalgh and Keith Negus (2002) outlines the history and development of popular music studies. Dan Laughey's (2006) *Music and Youth Culture* focuses especially on young listeners and their practices. Simon Frith's (2007) latest *Taking Popular Music Seriously* includes several of Frith's classic essays on popular music studies. Richard Peterson's comprehensive yet scholarly *Creating Country Music: Fabricating Authenticity* (1997), Tia DeNora's (2000) *Music in Everyday* Life, and Deena Weinstein's classic *Heavy Metal: A Cultural Sociology* (1991), and Herman, Sloop and Swiss's, *Mapping the Beat* (1997) are very specific, in-depth analyses. All of these texts—and there are others—treat popular music as an important social product with deep consequences for social structure, selfhood, and culture. We intend to locate our work in this tradition.

Our purpose and approach mark an important difference between our book and other texts. This concise textbook is organized in terms of conventional sociological topics and is oriented to the needs of two precisely defined audiences. The first audience is made up of undergraduate students of introductory sociology, for which the textbook is meant as a supplemental text. Each chapter is tied to a traditional topic in introductory sociology. We use popular music to illustrate fundamental social institutions, theories, sociological concepts, and processes, and we are the first to do so in the hope of drawing our readers into the fascinating and ever-relevant world of sociology. We write with confidence that reading and thinking about popular music will open up class discussions, debate, and reflection on the power of sociological study and the importance of a sociological imagination. The second audience is made up of students of courses in the sociology of popular music. The uniqueness of our book for that audience comes from our placing popular music within the complex and ever-changing context of everyday life. We hope that both audiences benefit from our accessible language, our use of diverse and contemporary data from the world of popular music and popular culture, and our personable tone. We also expect both audiences will also benefit from our concentration on U.S. and Canadian musical and social phenomena. Thus, while much of the literature on popular music studies takes a rather UK-centric approach, we primarily focus on the new continent.

Regardless of audience considerations, the essential principle of this textbook is that popular music is one of the most important sources of culture in our society. Popular music provides the soundtrack for everyday life while providing practical meanings for making sense of everyday life. Accordingly, the textbook is organized to accomplish two instructional objectives. First, we show how popular music affects all major social institutions. Second, we show how popular music can be used to illustrate fundamental sociological theories and concepts. In other words, we are using a social phenomenon of great interest to students to draw them in, to bring life to their/your study of sociology.

In what follows we pay attention to the intersections between popular music and the family, religion, socialization, ideology, social and political organization, the economy, culture and subcultures, self and identity, race, class, gender, technology, deviance, and globalization— only to mention some of the material contained in the pages to come. Throughout, we hope to connect individual and group-based conduct, feelings, and thought with cultural rituals, values, norms, texts and performances, all within contexts shaped by historical, geographic, economic, political, and socio-linguistic relations. Aware that it is impossible for anyone to know everything about sociology, just as it is impossible for anyone to know everything about music, we hope that by bringing these two passions of ours together, we can share a bit of our sociological and musical imagination with you.

This textbook is derived, not only from our personal interests in music, but also in our teaching and scholarly research on popular music. Joe has taught undergraduate and graduate courses in the sociology of popular music at the University of Houston for seventeen years. He is a scholar in the field of the sociology of everyday life and of popular culture and a founding member of the Sociology of Music Network, sponsored by the Culture Section of the American Sociological Association. He has conducted research and published essays on popular music topics including the postmodernization of rock music, as exemplified by the popularity of Metallica; punk, heavy metal and Christian heavy metal club scenes; and the rave movement and designer drug use. Joe recently collaborated on a team project, funded by the U.S. National Institute on Drug Abuse, examining the multi-faceted use of Internet-based support groups by designer drug users. He is currently conducting a comprehensive ethnographic study of the various Latino music scenes in Houston, funded by the Joseph Werlin Foundation. His on-going research on baby boomer rock 'n' roll fans will appear in *Growing Old with Rock 'n' Roll*, to be published by Left Coast Press in 2009. He enjoys music from his youth, especially the Rolling Stones and later Van Morrison, music he shares with his children (e.g. Mozart), and music he shares with his wife (e.g. Sting and Paul McCartney).

Phillip teaches popular music in relation to cultural theory, media and cultural studies. A sociologist by training and a communication and cultural studies scholar by vocation, he has examined a range of cultural phenomena, ranging from the value of authenticity in music, to cultural representations of the popular self and youth culture. His theoretical focus in terms of popular music is on developing models for the practical ways people use music in everyday life. One of his most recent pieces is the application of the logic of music to understanding the logic of social interaction. He has also published essays on Avril Lavigne, Britney Spears, the indie-rock produced by Constellation Records, and the genre of teen pop. Phillip is very picky about his music. He loves progressive hardcore punk, space rock, grunge (yes, still) and music with roots in his local beloved environment of Vancouver Island, British Columbia.

The present text evolved from a previous collaboration. In 2006, Joe and Phillip co-edited a special issue of the sociological journal *Symbolic Interaction*. The topic was popular music, and the contributions reflected both the enthusiasm and the sophistication of the study of popular music through an interactionist perspective. Papers included discussions of the jazz music scene; grotesque rock music, such as the Marilyn Manson phenomenon; and the work of the hip hop DJ. This work produced the idea—leading to the design of this text—that the sociology of popular music had evolved to the point where it could and should make an impact of the ways we understand and teach sociology in general.

We are both sociologists of everyday life. That means that we study, teach, and write about the ways people deal with practical problems in very practical ways. The "stuff" that we observe and use as data are *social meanings* (Kotarba and Johnson 2002), that is, the rules, values, rituals, customs, understandings, and experiences that people use on a daily basis to make sense of the world in which they live. Therefore, the topics we choose to examine in our work and to discuss in this text are topics that are important to the people for whom popular music is a key source of meaning for their lives. Sociologists of everyday life are often pegged as "micro-sociologists." Micro-sociologists, some believe, study small groups of people in precisely defined contexts while neglecting to take into consideration greater historical, political, or economic trends. Whereas we do focus on the study of cultural processes at the level of narrowly situated contexts, we in actuality pay close attention to "bigger," and "macro" sociological issues. In fact, as we explain in the Introduction, we combine our "micro" constructivist approach with a critical theoretical sensitivity. Yet, in doing so, we continue to privilege the study of music from the perspective of those who listen to it, rather than from some kind of opinionated, dismissive, and arrogant standpoint. Being sociologists of everyday life, we aim to explain and understand first and foremost rather than to criticize first.

The term *ethnographic tourism* (Kotarba 1984) pretty much summarizes the way we study popular music in everyday life. Our work is ethnographic to the degree that it attempts to describe popular music in terms of the natural situations in which it occurs, and in terms of the language, feelings and perceptions of the individuals who experience it. The metaphor of tourism applies in the following way. Most sociological research occurs in the researcher's own land. The researcher assumes that the phenomenon (or features of the phenomenon) in question are to be explored, since they are hidden by a background of an otherwise familiar, taken-for-granted, and immediately plausible world. The researcher identifies cases for analysis through strategic but systematic sampling. He then proceeds to venture into a territory to observe everything that goes on, while preparing oneself to describe these realities for later storytelling before academic audiences. This logic fits best when the phenomenon in question is relatively rare (e.g., deviant behavior or minority group behavior) or particularly curious due to its strangeness, uniqueness, and potential for revealing larger social issues.

When the researcher assumes that the phenomenon in question is everywhere, then he or she should act like a stranger or tourist in a foreign land. No setting should be taken for granted. Indeed the researcher should act like a foreigner in one's own land in order to *observe* the phenomenon where it was previously ignored by both researchers and members of the culture at large. The world of everyday life and popular music fits this scenario well. Our primary research strategy involves observation of ordinary, everyday life activities of ordinary people, musical performances, personas, texts, rituals, and music-related objects. As we further discuss in the Introduction, our ethnographic tourist strategy thus does not stop where a conventional tourist might (at the surfaces only), or where a conventional ethnographer of foreign culture might (at the depths only). Through the use of our own sociological imagination we engage in a continuous back and forth play between depths and surfaces, supplementing observation and description with interpretation, and interpretation with evidence. And we hope to have some fun while doing this too, not unlike a tourist would.

We did not work alone on this book. We enlisted the assistance of students in our undergraduate and graduate courses in the sociology of popular music/rock and roll, and media and popular culture studies. They not only helped us learn about other people's musical experiences, shared their rich musical experiences with us, and helped to further reflect on our tastes and ideas, but ultimately . . . hey; they're college students like you and they helped us learn about the latest trends and your culture! We also make good use of data or information derived from observations and reflections on our musical experiences as well as those of our families—all rock and roll fans. We also bene-fited from the gracious help of our editor at Routledge, Steve Rutter, and our reviewers, who helped us to clarify our ideas, stay on task, and organize our thoughts. Just like music, a book too is a collective social product.

At the same time a book is also, similar to a musical performance, an individual product. While melodies are the outcomes of collaboration and harmony, at times both musical performers and book authors do like to launch into a solo. This is more common in music, and less in academic writing. In music, we have the unmistakable funkiness of a guitar played by the unique talents of Tom Morello or Mike McCready, the unique grain of the voice of Janice Joplin or Tracy Chapman, and so forth. In academic writing, instead, most scholars prefer to surrender the potential for displaying their uniqueness and abide by the conven-tions of a formal tone. We instead prefer to write music like we would play music (not that we know how to play music at all, though, LOL!). Hence, while we always try and play as a duo (since we have edited each other's work, and since at times we speak in unison like we are doing right now) in the following chapters we often launch into solos. When-ever we do so we make it a point of letting you know who's speaking: either Joe or Phillip. And that's how you'll get to listen to Joe's own voice and way of speaking, with his unique Chicago-molded, California-influenced, Texas-style attitude. And that's also how you get to hear from Phillip, with his pungent European tone, his mellow West Coast moods, and his proud and unique Canadian rhythms. With our differences in age, lifestyle, background, and experience we try and bring you the product of our unique individual selves and emergent collaboration: both the solos and the harmony that make music (and sociology) an individual and social product.

INTRODUCTION: THE SOCIOLOGY
OF POP(ULAR) MUSIC

A traditional distinction in the study of music performance is that between popular music and classical music. Take the way such distinction operates in the context of teaching and learning, for example. One learns to play classical guitar or electronic guitar, one learns to sing or dance contemporary styles or classic, and one enrolls in university programs that make sharp distinctions between a classical curriculum and jazz. These two worlds of music cannot seem more distant. Yet, as sociologists we must remain skeptical of all classifications. Classifications are not simply convenient ways of separating things that are essentially different (that is, different in and of themselves), but instead practices that create and reinforce differences that we impute to things ourselves. Take, for example, classical music consumption. One can purchase a classical music CD through the same online or shopping mall retailers that sell popular music, often for the very same price of those latter recordings. One can listen to classical music as white noise in the background of one's office or car engine humdrum much like one would do with less high-brow music. One can even use one's "membership," that is one's allegiance, to a classical music world to distinguish one's taste from other classical and non-classical music "fans," not unlike a snobby indie-rocker might do. Even classical music distribution is similar to popular music distribution, being in the hands of few large-scale corporations, like Naxos, whose blurred repertoire, marketing, distribution, and direct retail practices make the classical music–popular music distinction a notion of the past. In light of all this, what is "popular" music?

If we agree that the word popular more or less means "of the

1

people," then popular music is the music preferred by the people (that is, a good number of them). Following this argument, if many people today—and therefore not only and no longer a hyper-privileged, "cultured," upper-class and aristocratic-like minority—enjoy classical music, is classical music not popular music as well? The answer would have to be an absolute "yes." So, there we are: left with little distinction between classical and popular music, at least in terms of the sociological dimensions we have taken into consideration. In light of this we can state that the general aim of sociological music studies is to examine the social aspects of the production, distribution, and consumption of *popular* music. Because all of music is equally produced, distributed, or consumed by people, and because sociology examines people's interactions of all kinds, sociologists of popular music are equally well prepared for dealing with all aspects of the study of music, any kind of it, as a social product.

At this point some of you may feel a good degree of satisfaction knowing that distinctions—such as those between high-status musical styles like opera and low-status musical styles like surf rock—are arbitrary, politically-motivated *social constructions.* You might even be thinking about facebooking that high school classical music teacher that looked down on your Mohawk and remind him of that. On the other hand, some of you may recognize that despite the arbitrariness of any objective or universal hierarchy of values between musical expressions some differences among them do indeed exist. After all, you can't just show up for a night at the opera theater with your surfboard, for example. And your typical operagoer, no matter how "local" he/she is claims to be, wouldn't be allowed to surf your waves and share your surf rock on the beach in his/her sharply pressed tuxedo. In fact, while distinctions are always more or less ideological, in practice, they do work. Another way of saying this—following the pragmatist tradition—is that reality may be a matter of conventions and ideas, but those conventions and ideas are really meaningful in their consequences. Such is the basic idea behind the meta-theoretical paradigm known as *constructivism* or *social constructionism*: the very starting point of our introduction to this book.

CONSTRUCTIONIST THEORETICAL PERSPECTIVES IN THE SOCIOLOGY OF POP MUSIC

Introductions to sociology textbooks generally survey three bodies of sociological theory: conflict, functionalist, and interactionist theories. Introductions to the sociological study of popular music like this one generally utilize—but for the most part only implicitly—instead *critical* and *constructionist* approaches. This is important stuff, so let's make some sense of all this. To make things simpler right off the bat, let's put aside functionalist theory. Few contemporary scholars of popular music adopt functionalist theories, and given our own approach to this book, it is safe to say that functionalism will matter little in this context. So, one down and two up: conflict theory and interactionism. Let us deal with interactionism first.

Interactionist scholars of popular music generally pay attention to the meanings that people attribute to music, to how people act toward one another in relation to music and toward music in relation to their social ties. Symbolic interactionists are really not the only ones who do this, though. Ethnomethodologists, dramaturgists, phenomenologists, and other micro-sociologists and some sociologists of culture prefer to study popular music as a meaningful set of practices, performances, texts, and social world. In doing so they focus on what people do together with music and with one another. And because their analytical attention is on "doing," that is, on practice, action, conduct, behavior, rituals, work, and in the consequences of ideas, values, roles, scripts, language, and norms, they are generally said to be *constructionists*. Constructionism is therefore an umbrella category for a number of theories which include symbolic interactionism and others.

A constructionist is someone who believes that social realities are *made* by people acting in accord with (and often in spite of) one another. In making social realities, people attribute meaning, assign value, classify, distinguish, rank, discriminate, and so forth. In the case of music, constructionists explain, for example, how genres take shape; how people shape, follow, and abandon the musical fashions they have created; how people construct a sense of identity, individual and collective, around music; how family members socialize one another to appreciate and understand musical traditions; how musical performances unfold as symbolic rituals; how the forms of organization of music subcultures are shaped on the basis of what people do in each other's co-presence, and so forth. In sum, a social constructionist takes an attitude toward the social world not unlike the attitude that a construction worker takes toward a building: they both understand that the final product is the emerging and uncertain result of cooperation and struggle, strategy, skill, resources, organization, negotiated expectations, ideas, and most importantly interpersonal action (after all you can't build a skyscraper from scratch alone, right?).

Traditionally, within sociology, constructionists have belonged to the group of micro-sociologists, but things have been changing. Today, and for the past twenty years or so, constructionist and interactionist ideas have flourished all over sociology. Trends like these are blurring the boundaries between perspectives, and thus it is no longer uncommon for a sociologist to be doing constructionist research with a critical and conflict-oriented bend, or for a critical scholar to be using constructionist ideas. Indeed, even we like to mix critical and constructionist ideas together in the pages to follow. So, now that we have explained what constructionism is, and asserted that it generally blends well with critical theory, let us examine critical theory.

To begin with, critical theory is not synonymous with conflict theory, yet critical theory has emerged from conflict theory. Conflict theory was born out of the writings of Karl Marx and his immediate and more orthodox followers. Critical theory is instead more closely associated with the Frankfurt School of Critical Theory first, and then with the University of Birmingham's Contemporary Centre for Cultural Studies (henceforth, CCCS). It is especially the latter institution which, in the late 1970s and 1980s, renewed sociological and interdisciplinary interest in critical theory, in popular culture and popular music studies, and in the potential of a uniquely constructionist and critical agenda. It did so by downplaying the role of the economy in society. For Marx, capital-based relations accounted for the entire structure of social organization. But for his critical followers of the Frankfurt School, the economy instead, while a strong force, was not the only social force to be reckoned with, and certainly was not omnipotent as Marx envisioned it. Thus, while they maintained their critical stance towards social inequality, they toned down their emphasis on how those fixed those inequalities are. If one were interested in simplifying things a bit, one might say that critical theory differs from pure Marxist conflict theory because it incorporates a bit of the constructionist perspective. Such blending is nowhere more obvious than in the CCCS tradition.

The CCCS's heritage is an important one for current sociology. First, scholars at the CCCS followed the footsteps of earlier Frankfurt School critical theorists in pushing the agenda for a newer Marxism and conflict perspective that was more sensitive to people's abilities to act in collaboration with one another and change social realities. Second, in investigating the activities of youths, members of subcultures, and music followers, these scholars combined the earlier interests of the Chicago School of sociology in urban cultures with the critical sensibility of conflict and critical theory. And third, in showing the arbitrary yet politically rooted hierarchy of distinctions between high-brow culture and low-brow culture, these scholars brought to bear constructionist ideas in the dismantling of distinctions among cultures; for them in fact, just like for most cultural anthropologists, culture was not a matter of refinement and high-class taste and education but more simply a particular but mundane way of life.

Now, a lot of theory consumed all at once can give anyone a stomach ache, so let us step back a bit for a second and go back to popular music. Let us imagine a character, a guy or girl like many others. Let's give this character a name: Cameron. Cameron lives in Seattle. Not just any Seattle but the Seattle of the early 1990s. Yeah, the grungy one! Cameron looks like many youths around town: jeans, a Mother Love Bone concert t-shirt and a hooded sweatshirt, disheveled look, mellow attitude yet politically aware and more or less involved in environmental issues and other social causes. Cameron has a particular taste in music and is a huge music buff: grunge, indie-rock, anything heavy with the exception of glam, butt-rock type guitar music. Cameron is also growing up. Maybe wondering a bit about the future and worrying about paying bills and eventually having to settle down with a ballooning student loan debt. Cameron works odd days at Kinko's, takes classes at Seattle Central Community College, drives his beat-up Nissan every other weekend to catch some good shows down in Olympia— and occasionally plays base guitar with some Evergreen State College friends—and every now and then parties downtown at the Crocodile. A pretty normal life, right? So, why does Cameron matter to us?

Cameron matters to us as sociologists of popular music because his/her identity (among other things) cannot be understood without a comprehension of the role that music plays in his/her life. Only by focusing on the meanings that Cameron attributes to music, by paying attention to how that music allows Cameron to cement social ties with friends, to understand the politics of the world, to express emotionality and so forth, can we hope to understand Cameron a bit better. To do this, we need to put ourselves in Cameron's shoes. We need to do this in order to understand how she/he makes his/her world, how he/she attributes meaning to it. In other words, we need to become ethnographic tourists in Cameron's life. We need to hang out with Cameron, listen to his/her stories, and see life from his/her perspective. This is what generally a constructionist does. A constructionist follows *interpretive* approaches to studying the world, approaches that allow for a thick description of Cameron's (and others') social world, approaches that rely on the use of qualitative and humanist data. Yet, a full understanding of Cameron's life with music might require something else.

To put Cameron's life in perspective, we might need to understand his/her social position. As a grunge fan, Cameron has already engaged in a bit of social positioning of his/her own, whether she/he is aware of this or not. In its early stages grunge emerged as a form of protest music: protest against the growing standardization of youth culture, against the superficiality of popular culture, against both the consumerism and excessive hedonism of the music of the 1980s, and against the idealistic and utopian values of the hippie generation that preceded it. Cameron's musical identity might then very well be understood as a battle cry born out of social angst: angst toward his/her biographical particulars (such as growing up in a quickly expanding and increasingly wealthy city) and angst towards the general political marginalization of youth culture and youth issues by the political system. And this is what a critical approach to social/musical issues does: it attempts to understand the meanings of musical choices, discourses, and practices by critically reflecting on social positions and on the stratification of social positions. It focuses on those particular historical and political discourses, musical (and other) texts, and practices through which social positions can be created and expressed, and through which hierarchies and inequalities can be highlighted and criticized.

Together, the constructionist and critical approach make for a very thorough understanding of the social dimensions of everyday life. Without pretending to speak for others—without having first undertaken to see the world from their eyes—a sociology of popular music that is grounded in an everyday life approach speaks about others and the self of the writer as well. And it does so with a very keen focus on matters of culture. Indeed, one might say that the scope of such a sociological analysis is similar to the work of a cultural interpreter insofar as we learn about the culture of a social world (like that of Cameron's life) and write about that culture for another culture altogether: the culture of sociologists, students of sociology, and any reader interested in social issues. Given the importance of a firm understanding of culture, let us work toward a clarification of that idea.

MUSIC AND CULTURE

Culture is a way of life. Despite the fact that some people refer to culture as an ensemble of artistic practices, folk customs, and educational background, sociologists and other social scientists view culture differently as a system of symbolic meanings and a variety of processes of formation, exchange, and use of those meanings. When we understand culture as a way of life we become sensitized to seeing the presence of culture everywhere. This is why as sociologists of everyday life we feel particularly keen on attempting to understand and explain the most taken for granted and minute cultural expressions. Rather than explaining the concept of culture further by providing additional definitions, let us try to capture the uniqueness of the culture of our times by returning to our earlier example.

To anyone who has lived their life much earlier in the twentieth century, Cameron's life would seem full of choices. Cameron didn't have to take a job at Kinko's, to choose to drive an old and beat-up Nissan, or to go to school to Seattle Central Community College. As a matter of fact, Cameron—being from North Bend, outside of Seattle— didn't have to move to the city. Music too is a choice. And the choice for Cameron is endless. Any shelves of any music store offer a vast choice of musical styles: country, heavy metal, R & B, rap, classical, industrial, etc. Cameron's choice to abandon religion in his/her early teens is also a choice. Clothing style is also a choice. We could continue on and on, but you get the point that we are making: if there is one distinguishing characteristic of the way of life of our times it is that we have an unprecedented amount of choice. Ask your grandparents, if you can, about their choices when they were your age, like how many recordings they could choose from at the "music store." You'll get a different picture. And they'll get a good laugh out of your question. They'll laugh *with* you, of course.

Musical choices are cultural choices. After all music is part of the way we choose to live our life. And if it is a culture of choice that we speak of, then perhaps we need to wonder what the deeper consequences of choosing are. Sociologist Anthony Giddens (1991) writes that never before has Western culture been so receptive to the power of choice. Indeed, who we ourselves are, as individuals, is a matter of choice. Our self is a project of sorts. Cameron, in fact, could very well decide to trade in his/her grunge rock CD collection for some rap music, sell back his/her clothes at Value Village and buy Hammer-style parachute pants, and move to Los Angeles too. The following month, or year, Cameron could start over, with another identity of choice. You could too. We could too. The reason why we don't change all the time is because change and the very possibility of change provoke some anxiety in all of us. Anxiety, doubt, and fearing the loss of any sort of grounding or safety net are the necessary counterparts of a culture rich in choices and in the power of choosing. Cameron's angst comes in part from being a member of a generation that—perhaps more than any other generation before—has felt the freedom to choose. Angst, thus, comes in Cameron's case from the absence of firm traditions: the traditions that your grandparents and especially great-grandparents will tell you about if you ask them about their choices.

Some sociologists have decided to assign a moniker to the culture we have described: *postmodern*. By postmodern culture they mean a culture in which one's way of life is less grounded in traditions and more in choices, less grounded in certainties and more in doubts. A postmodern culture is marked by the seemingly endless availability of choice: fragmented musical styles, endless stimulation from multiple mass media of communication, the explosion of consumption and consumerism, the increased interconnectedness of the globe. Many more characteristics could be mentioned and many discussions could be opened. Yet, for the sake of brevity simply understand this: Cameron's sense of self and identity and Cameron's way of life have the quality of an open project in a way that is more distinctly so than any other time in modern history. Sociologists who believe in the truth of this statement are known as postmodernists. Elements of postmodern theory, and references to postmodern culture, occasionally ooze all over our insights throughout this book, and hopefully now you will know what we mean by that ever contentious expression: postmodernism.

To conclude this section let us reflect on an element of our example that we have ... er ... chosen to neglect: the limitations and costs of choices. Let us return to our example. Cameron's choice to become a grunge rock fan may seem arbitrary and inconsequential at first, but it is in actuality quite the opposite. Choices are hardly ever random. So if we spoke to Cameron we might learn that he/she was never intending on becoming who he/she is. Yet, lack of educational opportunities in his hometown made it more or less necessary to move to Seattle. Some of his/her high school friends were in the same position, so moving to a city was not only a necessity in relation to education but also represented the opportunity to maintain social networks. Cameron might also tell us that the choice for a college was more or less forced by limited opportunities. Many of Cameron's friends' parents were able to fund study at Evergreen State College for their children. Cameron instead had to take a job at Kinko's to help pay for tuition. That took time away from playing in a rock band. It also made Cameron resentful, politically motivated, and particularly sensitive to the appeal of lyrics like those of "Hunger strike" by Temple of the Dog:

> I don't mind stealing bread
> From the mouths of decadence
> But I can't feed on the powerless
> When my cups are already overfilled
> But it's on the table
> The fire is cooking
> And they're farming babies
> While the slaves are working
> The blood is on the table
> And their mouths are chocking
> But I'm growing hungry

Sociologists of everyday life such as ourselves, as critical construction-ists and postmodernists, might then suggest that choice exists but it is *structured* or limited by several characteristics of the very social struc-tures which enable ways of life and the amount of choice therein. Music, and musical cultures, are then serious sociological business, business which allows us to understand a great deal about society and social theory in general: the very scope of this book. Even though by now it seems obvious to you that studying popular music is a very useful and smart way of understanding social relations, this was not always the case. In the next section we briefly review the recent history of the study of music within sociology and a little bit of the history of sociology itself.

A VERY BRIEF HISTORY OF THE STUDY OF POP MUSIC IN SOCIOLOGY

Since we have more or less erased the boundaries between popular music and classical music for the sake of subjecting both of those to sociological analysis, let us demarcate our territory—that is, the precise field that we explore in this book—by choosing an expression that captures the identity of the diverse types of music on which we focus here. Let us choose the expression "pop music." Pop music is then intended to refer here to all types of music that are not classical music.

Please note: we use several terms or labels for musical styles that, hopefully, are not too confusing. *Popular* or *pop music* is the most general category we will analyze. Pop music refers to all styles of music that is mass produced, mass marketed, and in generally treated as a commodity in our North American societies. *Rock 'n' roll* refers to that style of popular music that emerged after World War II as a distinct feature of youth culture. Rock 'n' roll is loud, fast, guitar-driven, typic-ally amplified, very danceable, and oriented towards young—e.g., teen-aged—audiences. *Rock* refers to more contemporary versions of rock 'n' roll. *Jazz, rap, dance,* etc. are other styles of popular music.

We can ordinarily think of pop music as emerging during the early twentieth century when music became an economic commodity in our society, to be produced and marketed like any other consumable goods. There were two technological events that fueled this phenomenon. First, the advent of radio in the 1920s brought music into the homes of millions of North Americans. Perhaps the major impact of radio on music was its ability to present new and different styles of music beyond the classical, family, church and community-based music to which people were accustomed previously. Second, the advent of recorded music, in a period that critical theorist Walter Benjamin

([1936] 1969) referred to as the *age of mechanical reproduction*, turned music into a personal possession—with a price tag—that could be experienced and enjoyed at will, that could be distributed widely, and which could make music a lucrative business for producer, composer, and musician alike.

Much of the early scholarly work on popular music, including that of the Frankfurt School, was written from a critical, if not elitist, perspective. Theodore Adorno (1949), for example, frowned on jazz (his expression for what we call "pop music") as a low-status form of music that elicited non-rational, animalistic responses from its fans, in contrast to classical music that supposedly elevated one's mind and spirit. In addition, early critical thinkers like Adorno felt that capitalists marketed popular music to anesthetize the working class politically and to increasingly subjugate them economically.

In recent years, cultural scholars, including sociologists, have been much friendlier to pop music. These writers were largely baby boomers themselves who were raised not only on pop music, but on rock 'n' roll music specifically. To them, pop music is a fundamental force in North American and—increasingly global—culture, to be appreciated as well as understood. Later generations of scholars who went through their youth in the late 1960s, 1970s, and 1980s felt very similar to their baby-boomer predecessors. The sociology of music then became overwhelmingly the sociology of pop music. We argue that there have been four moments in the sociological analysis of pop music that closely parallel the historical development of pop itself in western society over the past fifty years. We will briefly describe these four moments in order to understand the evolution of both social phenomena. The key theme that we emphasize in the next paragraphs is that the sociology of pop music has generally focused in its earlier years on rock 'n' roll. With the growing diversification of rock and multiplication of styles that originate in but deviate from rock, the sociology of pop music has become more diversified as well.

The first moment of rock 'n' roll occurred during the 1950s, when youth culture as we know it was born. We are acknowledging, of course, the fact the cultural and musicological roots of rock 'n' roll can be traced back at least several decades (Friedlander 1996). It was during the 1950s, however, that rock 'n' roll received its name and dramatically entered North American everyday life and parlance. Interestingly, early sociological views on youth culture in general and rock 'n' roll specifically were quite positive and supportive of this cultural movement. James Coleman (1961) conceptualized rock 'n' roll as *youth culture*. He observed, through his massive study of American high schools that early rock 'n' rollers like Elvis Presley and Buddy Holly provided a soundtrack for helping the community manage the burgeoning population of teenagers resulting from the success of the emerging middle-class family (1950s and 1960s). The growing varieties of popular music in the 1950s helped socialize young people into their "appropriate" social classes. Coleman saw rock 'n' roll as the soundtrack for working-class youth. In many ways, early scholarly writing on rock 'n' roll discovered this music as it was already understood and experienced by its fans.

The second moment of rock 'n' roll occurred during the late 1960s and 1970s. Rock 'n' roll music grew to become a cultural entity much greater than the beat for sock hops or the drive-in. It took on broader political implications through its links to the civil rights and anti-war movements. In the second moment, sociologists like Simon Frith (1981) and George Lewis (1983) conceptualized rock 'n' roll as *popular culture*. They focused on rock 'n' roll music as the product of the popular culture industry in capitalistic society. They also acknowledged the fact that the rock 'n' roll audience was much more diverse than the notion of "youth" implies. Experientially, there were white, black, gay, men's and women's rock and roll(s) and, subsequently, markets.

The third moment occurred in the 1970s and 1980s when rock 'n' roll lost some of its critical appeal and became increasingly entrenched in and controlled by the entertainment industry. The ensuing revolt against corporate rock 'n' roll, especially in terms of the new wave and punk movements in England, led British scholars such as Dick Hebdige and other writing from the Birmingham School to conceptualize rock 'n' roll as *subculture*. They examined the political nature of rock and other styles as subversive voices of working-class teenagers, especially in Great Britain. These scholars advanced the methodologies used to study rock 'n' roll from classic survey research to semiotics. This approach fit the objective of understanding how audiences define and integrate music into their already constituted realities (i.e., social class memberships). Thus, the working-class punk subculture appropriated elements of upper-class culture, like dress, and used them to ridicule and criticize the life of the rich and powerful.

In the fourth moment of the 1980s and 1990s, sociologists joined other scholarly observers to conceptualize rock 'n' roll as *culture*. They saw rock 'n' roll as simply one feature of a postindustrial or post-modern culture undergoing radical transformation. The generational boundaries that so obviously delineated youth from their parents were cracking. Lawrence Grossberg (1992), for example, proclaimed the death of rock 'n' roll insofar as it no longer functions to empower teenagers by differentiating them from their parents and other adults. By the time we entered the 1990s, cross-generational pop music that could be enjoyed by everyone had started to supplant rock 'n' roll as the dominant soundtrack in American culture. Rap music has taken over much of rock 'n' roll's political role. Yet, rock 'n' roll has not simply died. In the spirit of the postmodern era in which we live, rock 'n' roll has dissolved into the pastiche of popular music that results in white rappers like Eminem, rock and rapper groups Limp Bizkit, and pop acts such as Shakira and John Legend. MTV and VH1 in the United States and Much Music and Much More Music in Canada have been major media forces in creating this cultural gumbo. As E. Ann Kaplan (1987) has noted, MTV is a reflection of the pervasiveness of the visual dimension of postmodern culture, as rock 'n' roll has been absorbed by the overwhelming power of the television medium on which teenagers have been raised.

Therefore, rock 'n' roll is no longer synonymous with popular music, but should be seen as one facet of the increasingly complex musical and cultural phenomenon known as popular music. Age is one factor in this growing complexity. Amid all these changes taking place in popular music and the entertainment industry's search for new audiences and ways to provide music to them, we witness numerous ways in which adults are increasingly present and relevant to rock 'n' roll and pop music. Beatles CD compilations have been among the highest selling music at Christmas for many years. Middle-aged fans pay hundreds of dollars to sit in the "Gold Circle" seats at the Eagles and Who concerts, where they sip white wine instead of the Boones Farm of their college days many years ago. The summer concert "shed" scene would be very thin without sold-out Moody Blues, Chicago, Kansas, Paul Simon, James Taylor, Ringo Starr, Sting/Police and Reo Speedwagon stops. Why have so many adults not outgrown rock 'n' roll? Why do innumerable teenagers angrily shout to their parents to "turn that noise down" when mom and dad are grooving to an old Rolling Stones CD? Why do so many adults continue to operationalize "Popular Music" in terms of the rock 'n' roll idiom with which they grew up?

In a very postmodern way, the continuing fourth moment of rock 'n' roll will continue to defy earlier patterns of performance, consumption, and style. We can safely say that we are in fact moving into a fifth moment of pop music and pop music studies within sociology. The fifth moment is a typically postmodern one: marked by extreme diversification of both musical offer and sociological offer, by increasing doubt over the authenticity of pop music, by a loss of musical tradition (like rock 'n' roll) accompanied by a nostalgic and pastiche-like recovery of the past, and by the increasing global fusion of styles and blurring of differences. Sociologically, this translates in a coming together of theoretical perspectives on the study of popular music, and an explosion in the sociological interest in popular culture. Indeed, as culture industries try and appeal to consumers by listening to their needs for diversity, so do the "sociological industries." And indeed our book too attempts to answer to the introductory student's need for diversity in pedagogical scope!

We will close with the following illustrative observation. On July 7, 2007, "Live Earth: The Concerts for a Climate in Crisis," consisted of ten concerts in eight countries that played to the largest music benefit crowd ever. There were numerous new artists that one might expect to be attractive to the youngest audience members, such as Wolfmother and Ludacris. Yet, perennial favorites Madonna, the Police, Bon Jovi and Melissa Etheridge—artists whom the parents of the youngest audience members made famous years ago—were presented as headliners. Their performances were, in fact, among the most spirited of all 257 performances on July 7, 2007. Old school rock 'n' roll as the new youth culture? Go figure.

CONCLUSION: CULTIVATING A MUSICAL AND SOCIOLOGICAL IMAGINATION

If we wish to understand the meanings of pop music and be critical of those cultural practices and values which result in the formation or re-creation of cultural injustices, we need to follow an approach to the study of our subject matter which is interpretive and critical at the same time. In doing so, we privilege methods and data that allow us to take the role and perspective of the people we intend to understand, that allow us to focus on the construction of meaning through language and language use, and that allow us to interpret the significance of music-related practices in a precise historical, political, geographical, and economic context. In our Preface we discussed our approach to the study of all this. We called it ethnographic tourism, and explained how it constitutes an example of the sociological study of everyday life. In this Introduction we have discussed our constructionist and critical perspective, explained how and why this perspective is best followed via the use of qualitative data, and how important it is to maintain a healthy skepticism towards all social facts. Much of what we have done constitutes an example of sociological imagination.

Critical and interpretive sociologist C. Wright Mills (1959) coined the expression "sociological imagination" to refer to the ability to connect, by way of reflection, seemingly unconnected individual and social forces, and in particular biographical and historical issues. Sociology attempts to foster in all its publics—both students and stakeholders—a sociological imagination by getting them to reflect on the greater relevance of personal problems as social issues. Our focus on the study of pop music has precisely that objective in mind as well. Because few things matter to students as much as music does, we believe that by allowing students to reflect on the structuring of music as a social product we can introduce students to sociological theory and research. In doing so, we wish to focus in particular on three issues (cf. Mills 1959):

1. What is the structure of a particular musical social world and how does it differ from and compare to other actual and possible forms of social organization?
2. What are the key features of this musical social world, and what is its unique position and relation with greater historical processes?
3. What are the defining characteristics of men and women engaged in these musical social worlds and what goes on in their day-to-day lives?

By asking such questions, and by searching for answers to them, we can hope to understand behaviors as mundane as musical choices as outcomes of complex arrays of costs and opportunities for individual and collective action, and as deeply symbolic and meaningful acts. By understanding the links between individual biography and social history we can therefore comprehend the lives of individuals like Cameron and the historical and social contexts in which lives are lived. It is with this goal in mind, and by using music as a lens for doing this, that we write this book.

1

THE FAMILY

The family is one of the most important institutions in society and one of the most important topics in sociology. The family is what sociologists call a *primary group*, as it is among the groups who are most closely involved in the process of socialization of children to the adult world. We all live in families—whether by birth or by choice, or both—and our family lives are critical determinants of who we are, how we live, how we respond to situations in everyday life, and what our life chances (e.g., careers, health, and incomes) will turn out to be (Williams 1998). Families have cultures of their own, and increasingly borrow from the various cultures available in our contemporary social life to manage their everyday life affairs.

Following Burgess (1926: 5) we can define *"family"* as a "unity of interacting persons." Such a definition escapes, purposefully, criteria of legal or blood ties, and historical and cultural prescriptions. Defining family as a unity of interacting persons also allows us to focus on how families emerge as such unities, as well as on the roles associated with all the persons involved. When we focus on interacting individuals we also coincidently zero in on the main focus of this type of interaction: socialization. Formally defined *socialization* is the "continuous process of negotiated interactions out of which selves are created and re-created" (Gecas 1981: 165). Just like families, socialization never stops as we are constantly socialized—though at times more than others—to our society by virtue of sheer exposure to norms, values, roles, ideals beliefs, practices, etc. Families are, however, more central than most other groups to the socialization process because by virtue of interacting with parental figures a child acquires early on, and throughout a lifetime, key symbolic resources for the development of a sense of self. More on the self and the life course will be said later.

Not only do family interactions lead to the development of a self-concept, identities, values, beliefs, etc. but family interactions also contribute to nurturance and protection. Yet, even within a family household a child is not immune from external *socialization agents*, like the mass media, and like music. Indeed, lay and professional critics have long cast a wary eye to children's culture that has evolved in capitalistic society, largely as a result of the decreasing influence of parental figures, and the growing influence of media as a primary group. We can call these critics *moral entrepreneurs*: individuals who work toward the definition and enforcement of moral values (Becker 1963). Recently, some of these moral entrepreneurs have been especially critical of materials emanating from the electronic media. These materials include television violence (which allegedly leads to violent behavior among young viewers); music videos (some of which contain sexist or sexually promiscuous messages); and rap music (which is criticized for many reasons, including the promotion of criminal lifestyles and rampant materialism) (cf. Wilson 1989). Popular music has been critiqued most often and most harshly, being designated as a "social problem" ever since its inception over fifty years ago. The aim of this chapter is to qualify this argument by illustrating the positive functions of popular music within family settings (Kotarba 1994b).

MUSIC AS A SOCIAL PROBLEM?

Constructionists do not view social problems as objective conditions. *Social problems* are instead seen as outcomes of negotiations over the meaning and moral value of an event, a state of being, or a situation. Thus, stealing from an early definition by Fuller and Myers (1940: 320) we can say that "social problems are what people think they are and of conditions are not defined as social problems by the people involved in them, they are not problems to those people." To have a social problem, therefore, one needs first to work in concert with others—and perhaps in spite of those with opposing views—toward defining a subject matter as problematic and worthy of concern. That kind of work is known as *social problem work*. Social problem work is the work of moral entrepreneurs. Let us examine the kind of social problem work done by moral entrepreneurs in relation to family and popular music.

Popular music has now fully become an integral feature of North American culture. For three generations, popular music has functioned as a primary source of meaning and leisure time activity for young people. Since its inception in the 1950s, it has been associated with adolescents, and has thus become a medium for both understanding and critiquing the adolescent generation. Some of the earliest sociological observers of popular music, namely rock 'n' roll, focused on its positive functions for adolescent development. Talcott Parsons (1949) argued that the adolescent culture that emerged after World War II, including the rock 'n' roll scene, was a functional mechanism for the societal control of the energy of this burgeoning generation.

Another early study gives us food for thought on the social problem status of popular music. James Coleman (1961) conducted a now classic survey of adolescent attitudes and behaviors in various Northern Illinois communities in 1955. Coleman was interested in studying both the secondary school experience and adolescent status systems. Coleman found that rock 'n' roll was the most popular form of music among both boys and girls. Girls liked to listen to records or the radio more than boys, a phenomenon Coleman explains with the observation that boys had a wider variety of activities available to them. Nevertheless, both boys and girls used rock 'n' roll to learn prevailing values for gender roles. Girls used romantic ballads and fan club memberships to learn about boys, dating, and so forth. Boys used "less conventional" stars like Elvis Presley to learn about adventure and masculinity. Overall, Coleman (ibid.: 236) viewed rock 'n' roll positively, since "music and dancing provide a context within which (teenagers) may more easily meet and enjoy the company of the opposite sex." Many teen-agers were "passionately devoted" to rock 'n' roll (ibid.: 315).

These early sociological observations have, however, been lost in a sea of criticism of the impact of popular music on adolescents (Martin and Segrave 1988). This criticism began in the 1950s with dramatic efforts to eliminate rock 'n' roll. Organized burnings of Elvis Presley records because of their alleged association with sinfulness and sexuality were common in fundamentalist communities. In the 1960s, another coalition of moral entrepreneurs argued that rock 'n' roll music was unpatriotic, communistic and the cause of drug abuse. In the 1970s and 1980s, the criticism became organized and sophisticated. Middle-class activist organizations, like the Parents Music Resource Center (PMRC) led by Tipper Gore, opposed much popular music for its alleged deleterious effects on the health of young people. In the 1990s, we find several court cases in which the prosecution and the defense have attempted to legally link popular music, especially heavy metal, goth, and grunge, with suicide and criminal behavior (Hill 1992). Most notably, the infamous Columbine shooting massacre has been linked with the culture of Marilyn Manson fans.

Allan Bloom was among the most influential moral entrepreneurs (1987). He wrote one of the most elegant intellectual attacks on popular music. Bloom, a Professor of Social Thought at the University of Chicago, argued that American universities were in a state of crisis because of their lack of commitment to traditional intellectual standards. Bloom further argued that young people live in a state of intellectual poverty: "Those students do not have books, they most emphatically do have music" (ibid.: 68). Plato, Socrates, and Aristotle all viewed music as a natural mechanism for expressing the passions and preparing the soul for reason. According to Bloom, university students' overwhelming choice in music today, rock music, instead:

> has one appeal only, a barbaric appeal, to sexual desire—not love, not *eros*, but sexual desire undeveloped and untutored . . . young people know that rock has the beat of sexual intercourse . . . Rock music provides premature ecstacy and, is like the drug with which it is allied . . . But, as long as they have the Walkman on, they cannot hear what the great tradition has to say. And, after its prolonged use, when they take it off, they find they are deaf.
>
> (ibid.: 68–81)

In general, many moral entrepreneurs have viewed popular music as either a social problem or a major cause of other social problems.

We wish to propose a contrasting argument. We are not arguing that popular music does not have its shortcomings and undesired effects. Our purpose is to show, however, that listening to rock and pop music has multiple consequences, many of which are positive in light of the role they play in the socialization process and solidifying family relationships. The specific positive consequence to be discussed in this chapter is the many different ways music integrates families and serves as a bridge across generations. This generational bridge allows children, adolescents, and adults to share communication, affect, morality, ethics, and meanings. Later, we will refer to this generation bridge as a kind of role-making.

One major reason critics focus on the dysfunctions of popular music is because they ignore the increasingly obvious fact that it is pervasive in North American culture (Kotarba 2002b). We now have three generations who have grown up with popular music and for whom pop music is the preeminent form of music. It serves as the soundtrack for everyday life, providing the context for phenomena such as commercials, patriotic events, high school graduations, political conventions, and so forth. The positive experiences of pop music simply do not attract the attention of observers, such as journalists and social scientists, whose work is structured around the concept of "the problem." In order to understand the pervasiveness of pop music and its positive as well as negative functions, we propose to reconceptualize it as a feature of children's culture.

POP MUSIC AS A FEATURE OF CHILDREN'S CULTURE

One of the central foci of constructionist and especially interactionist research in relation to the family has to do with the role that family members play in socializing one another not only to culture, but also to subcultures, like youth culture. And, yes, you read correctly: we did say socializing one another. As interactionists we may view socialization as *reciprocal and multi-directional.* In other words, we do not believe that the only kind of socialization is done by parents and guardians unto their children, but also by children unto their parents. Think for example of the volume of music listening. How many times have your parents shouted at you to keep the volume down? Well, guess what? The minute you become a parent and you catch your kids listening to music one decibel higher than you're willing to tolerate, you will catch yourself telling them exactly what your parents have told you for years: "Turn it down!!!" Then, chances are, as soon as that sentence escapes your lips you will catch yourself thinking: "Goodness, I sound like my mom/dad!" In this particular case, your children will socialize you to your role and related responsibilities by way of *altercasting* you, that is, by casting you in a role you are supposed to observe. Just like parents socialize children to adult roles, children socialize parents to adult roles! Altercasting is one of the many ways people make roles in everyday life.

Role is a key sociological concept. A *role* can be defined as a part an individual plays within a social setting. A part has rights and duties associated with it, as well as a social status. You can think of a role in play, for example. Within a play, a role is performed by an actor, who plays a script regardless of his/her personality, idiosyncrasies, etc. This happens in everyday social settings as well; as you remember from our loud music example. Also within a play we have minor and starring roles, like we do in society. However, there are some differences between theatrical roles and more mundane ones. Roles in most theatrical productions are strictly enforced by a director, for example, whereas individuals in mundane settings have more power to manipulate their roles and those of others. Within a family we have multiple roles, ranging from parent and relative to child. Roles are also age-graded. A parent is not always just a parent, but the parent of a teenager, or a pre-teen, or a college child, and so forth. Now, with this said, let us return to the music and to how family members socialize one another into specific roles and music-centered age-cultures.

Our thinking posits pop music, especially rock 'n' roll styles, as a key element of youth culture. The concept "youth culture," which can be traced at least as far back as the works of Talcott Parsons (1949), is commonly used to denote those everyday practices conducted by adolescents which serve: (1) to identify them as a specific generational cohort, separate from children and adults; (2) as common apparatus for the clarification and resolution of conflict with adults; and (3) to facilitate the process of socialization or transformation into adulthood. Before we go much farther with our argument, let us reflect on the link between music and youth culture.

Conventional thinking isolates certain socio-economic-cultural developments since World War II to construct an explanation for the historically integrated, co-evolution of teenagers and rock and pop (Frith 1981). This theory argues that teen-agers were a product of the post-war family. The general cultural portrait of this family is one of middle-class aspiration if not achievement, suburban orientation, affluence, and consumption. Teen-agers in the 1950s comprised not only a demographic bulge in the American population, but also an economic force. Teen-agers are viewed as a product of the following formula: allowances + leisure time + energy + parental indulgence. Rock and pop music became an available and useful commodity to sell to teen-agers. The music could be readily duplicated, the themes could directly address the angst and adventure of adolescence, and the 45 rpm record could be disposable through the process of the Top 40. As the post-war generation grew into adulthood in the 1960s, they took the previously fun-filled rock 'n' roll and turned it into a medium for political dissent and moral/cultural opposition to the generation of their parents. But, as the baby boomers reached full adulthood, they traded in their passion for rock 'n' roll for country music and Muzak, leaving succeeding generations of teenagers to consume the hegemonic cultural pablum of formulaic pop and MTV (Grossberg 1987).

Yet, a powerful cultural experience like growing up with rock 'n' roll cannot simply be left behind by movement through the lifecycle, that is, by adults' socialization into their new, adult roles. One would reasonably expect to find at least some residual effects of rock 'n' roll on adult baby boomers. So, our argument is that if rock 'n' roll affected the way they dated, mated, and resisted, then one would reasonably expect rock 'n' roll music to shape the way they make their roles, that is, the way they work, parent, construct and service relationships, and in other ways accomplish adulthood. Through our findings and focus, we reveal that paradoxically the presence of rock 'n' roll in the lives of adults as well as adolescents can be discovered by locating it in the lives and culture of children. How is this possible?

Postmodern theory is a useful analytical framework for guiding the search for pop music in the nooks and crannies of everyday life. Postmodern theory reminds us that contemporary social life is mass mediated. Culture is less a reflection of some underlying, formal, firm, structural reality than it is an entity in its own right (Baudrillard 1983). Postmodernism allows the observer to see things not previously visible. For example, postmodernism recently has let us see gender as a critical factor in the process of writing history. Instead of gazing directly at the alleged facts of the past, postmodernism allows historians to focus on the process by which history itself is written. Similarly, postmodern theory lets the sociologist analyze cultural forms like rock 'n' roll as free-floating texts with their own styles of production, dissemination, interpretation, and application to everyday life situations. Therefore, at least hypothetically, rock 'n' roll is no longer (if it ever was) simply a reflection of the structural positions of adolescents in western societies, no longer a possession of youth. Rather, cultural items in the postmodern world become available to anyone in society for their individual and subcultural interpretation, modification, and socialization. Another way of saying this is that social roles are less rigid in a postmodern world. We now witness white, middle-class kids listening to and enjoying gangsta' rap music. We see Bill Clinton belting out a bluesy-groove on his tenor sax, first at his appearance on Arsenio Hall's television program during the Presidential campaign and, later at one of his inaugural parties. To see popular music as a feature of children's culture and a resource for socialization and for role-making within the contemporary postmodern culture helps us to see its presence in all generations in the family, regardless of birth cohort. The concept *children's culture* denotes those everyday practices: (1) used by children to interpret and master everyday life; (2) created, acquired, disseminated, and used by adults to construct and define parental relationships with children; and (3) ordinarily associated with children and childhood yet used by adolescents and adults to interpret, master, or enjoy certain everyday life situations.

What we wish to show and argue in the remainder of this chapter is that pop music serves as a symbolic tool for family members to cross boundaries generally associated with their roles as family members. In other words, music serves as a tool for role-making and thus for reciprocal socialization into generational cultures. Thus, for example, children socialize their parents to children's culture through music; parents socialize their children to their own age-specific generational culture. Furthermore, children experience popular music not only as children, but also as a way of learning about their parents' culture, and thus as resource for taking their roles. Similarly, adolescents experience popular music to extend childhood, and adults experience rock 'n' roll to relive childhood. We will now provide an inventory of popular music (and in particular rock 'n' roll) as a tool for reciprocal socialization, and for blending experiences across generations. We will emphasize those rock 'n' roll experiences most taken for granted by professional and lay observers alike, because those experiences function positively as elements of children's culture. We will conclude with a brief discussion of the contribution of this style of analysis to the social scientific literature on rock 'n' roll and a reflection on the status of popular music as a social problem.

Adolescents as Children

As mentioned above, standard wisdom on rock 'n' roll argues that it has functioned largely to establish adolescence as a distinct stage in the lifecycle. Furthermore, rock 'n' roll is seen as a weapon in conflicts between adults and adolescents. The mass media contribute to this overstated, over-romanticized view of rock 'n' roll and adolescence. The film *Footloose*, for example, portrays the plausible scenario in which fundamentally conservative, small-town adults view rock 'n' roll as an evil influence on their teen-agers. Rock 'n' roll is portrayed in the film as the gauntlet which forces teen-agers to choose between good and evil by choosing their parents or dancing. The rebellious imagery of Elvis Presley portrays a prevailing cultural myth that allies rock 'n' roll with youthful rebellion, unbridled sexuality, cross-ethnic intimacy, and a wide range of delinquent activities.

These cultural images support an ideological vision of youth culture that overemphasizes the independence, rebellion, and integration of teen-agers. A revisionist or postmodernist reading of this history finds much more diversity within youth culture. For every Elvis Presley fan in the 1950s and 1960s, there was an *American Bandstand* fan. *American Bandstand*, especially in its early days when it was broadcast live after school from Philadelphia, portrayed rock 'n' roll as a form of pop music, in much milder and more acceptable (to adults as well as teen-agers) ways. The kids on *American Bandstand* were "All-American" kids. They dressed modestly and neatly. They all chewed Beechnut gum, provided by the sponsor of the program. And, above all, they were extremely well behaved. The boys and girls, especially the "regulars," tended to match up as boyfriends and girlfriends, not as potentially promiscuous dates and mates. *American Bandstand* probably represented most teen-agers in American society at that time. And, teen-agers could not participate in activities like *American Bandstand* without the approval, if not support, of their parents. After all, someone had to drive the kids to the studio or at least give them permission and money to take the bus there, just as someone had to provide the television and permit watching *American Bandstand* at home.

Parents were and continue to be cautious supporters of their children's popular music activities. There is more of a tendency among parents to manage popular music as though their teen-agers are children who need to be nurtured and protected, rather than adolescents who must be controlled, sanctioned, and feared. For example, Joe's current research on heavy metal and rap music has found the continuation of three generations of ambiguous parental feelings of cautious support toward these styles of pop music. At a recent Metallica concert in Houston, numerous teenagers indicated that their parents did not approve of heavy metal music for various reasons (e.g., volume, distortion, immorality, and potential affiliation with evil like Satanism). Yet, these same parents carpooled their teenagers and friends to the Astrodome on a school day and, in most cases, bought or provided the money for tickets. A similar situation exists among African-American and Hispanic parents in terms of the popularity of rap music among their teenagers (Kotarba 1994b). Mass media-generated images of obstinate if not rebellious youth generally ignore the reflexive relationship between teenagers and their parents. As long as teenagers live at home as legal, financial, and moral dependants—that is, as children—their parents provide the resources for creating musical identities (e.g., allowances, free time, and fashionable hip hop clothing). Parents then respond to the identities they helped create by controlling, criticizing, sanctioning, and punishing their teenagers for living out their popular music-inspired identities—responding to them as if they were autonomous, responsible adults.

From the teenagers' perspective, popular music is commonly an extension of childhood experiences. The Summer of Love in 1967 is the case in point. Mass media accounts treat the Monterey Music Festival and Haight-Asbury as benchmarks in the emergence of the youth counter-culture. The Summer of Love marked the fulfillment of rock 'n' roll as an instrument of adolescent rebellion, within a context of heavy drug use, free love, and political liberation—a clash between young people's values and those of their parents. The media argue that the political events of the late 1960s institutionalized and radicalized the unbridled, individualistic and existentially youthful rebellion of the 1950s and early 1960s.

A revisionist, postmodernist reexamination of these events suggests that the innocence of middle-class, post-war, baby-boom childhood served as the primary metaphor for these young people. High status was attributed to the "flower child," whom the counter-culture posited as the innocent who simply rejected the oppression of the adult establishment. Women in the movement with high status were known as "earth mothers," who nurtured themselves and their peers through natural foods, folk arts, and the ability to roll good joints for the group. Whereas the mass media stress the centrality of Jimi Hendrix and Jim Morrison to the music of this period, more child-like songs like Peter, Paul and Mary's "Puff, the Magic Dragon" and Jefferson Airplane's "White Rabbit" (inspired by *Alice in Wonderland*) were at least as significant. The 1960s generation popularized the use of animation as a format for rock 'n' roll (e.g., the Beatles' "Yellow Submarine"). Perhaps most interesting to our argument is the way the 1960s generation drifted away from the adult world of commercialized and confined concert halls to the park-like atmosphere of the open air concert festival, where the audience could play with frisbees and other toys.

The baby boomer generation's attempts to maintain the feeling of childhood through rock 'n' roll extends into their encounter with adulthood. From the 1980s on, the baby boomer generation has been the strongest supporter of contemporary versions of the rock 'n' roll festival. Every large and most medium-sized cities now have what are referred to as "shed venues." These outdoor concert sites, such as Ravinia in Chicago, Wolf Trap in Washington, D.C., and the Mitchell Pavilion in Houston, serve as the setting for baby boomers to bring their blankets and their picnic baskets—and often their children and grandchildren—to hear concerts by New Age performers. New Age music, by the way, fits our broad definition of rock 'n' roll, if not as a genre at least as a concept. It is simply mellow, electronically amplified music appreciated by adults who want to extend their rock 'n' roll experiences, but who for physical or status/cultural reasons choose to give up the volume and anxiety of pure rock 'n' roll.

Adolescents today continue to experience rock 'n' roll *qua* children at play. In 1984, Van Halen's "Jump" was a very popular rock song. Many lay and professional critics of hard rock chose to interpret the song as an invitation to youthful suicide. It appeared that the kids did not. At the Van Halen concert held in the Summit in Houston that year, the fans—who appeared to range mostly from 14 to 17 years of age—let out a collective scream when Eddie Van Halen began the song with the now famous keyboard riff. At the chorus, when David Lee Roth shouted "Jump," 18,000 teenagers did just that: they all jumped up together like a bunch of little kids in the playground during recess.

Even the darker moments of rock 'n' roll have their child-like attributes. Some teenage fans experience heavy metal music as a mechanism for managing lingering, childhood anxieties. Metallica's "Enter Sandman" was a popular video on MTV during 1991–1992. As part of an ethnographic study of homeless teen-agers, Joe asked these kids to talk about their music. This particular video was very popular with them. Joe asked them specifically to interpret a very old, scary-looking man in the video. The street kids tended to see the man as a reflection of their own real nightmares, such as physically abusive parents and drug-infested neighborhoods. In a contrasting set of interviews with middle-class kids, Joe commonly heard them say that the man represented nightmares, but only the inconsequential nightmares children have and ultimately outgrow (Kotarba 1994b).

Children as Children

The pervasive mass media increasingly expose young children to popular music. The Teenage Mutant Ninja Turtle rock concert tour and Saturday morning television (e.g., the *M.C. Hammer* cartoon program) all focus on pre-adolescent audiences. Perhaps the best current example is the Hannah Montana phenomenon. Nor does it stop there. Several school supply companies are now marketing math and reading enhancement programs based upon popular music icons and idioms, such as the Schoolhouse Rock.

But beyond simple marketing, popular music informs our general cultural views of children. *Honey, I Blew Up the Kids* was a popular film comedy in 1992. The story line had a bumbling, scientist father mistakenly turning his infant into a colossus. As the child innocently marched down a boulevard in Las Vegas, he grabbed the large, neon-lit guitar from a music club and proceeded to pretend to play a rock 'n' roll song (a generic, rock-a-billy song was actually playing in the film's background). The guitar served as a toy for the baby. The imagery suggested the baby as adolescent, an absurdity that helped establish the overall absurdity of the story.

Young children can grasp rock and pop even when it is not intentionally produced for or marketed to them. When the pop band Los Lobos covered the 1950s hit "La Bamba," it became a hit among elementary school-aged children. Like many rock and pop songs, young kids find its simple lyrics silly and its beat fun to dance around to. As country music broadens its appeal by "crossing over" to rock and pop music audiences, it also creates an audience of children. Hannah Montana's father, country singer Billy Ray Cyrus, had a hit with "Achy Breaky Heart" that has remained a fun song for many children.

An interesting development in children-oriented pop music has been the Gorillaz phenomenon. The Gorillaz are an animated rock band that is like a cartoon, except that it is appreciated by adolescents and children alike. Its award-winning videos are animations, and several of its songs have been radio and MTV hits. Fans also have access to play figure toys for all the Gorillaz characters.

Adults as Children

Adults who grew up on rock 'n' roll may want to relive the fun, excitement or meaningfulness of their earlier music experiences. This can happen in two ways. First, adults may simply retrieve the past through nostalgia. In many cities, oldies or "classic rock" music stations are the most popular radio stations, catering to audiences approximately 24–45 years of age. Rock 'n' roll nostalgia also appears in the guise of circa 1950s and 1960s clubs. These clubs are often decorated in post-war diner motif, offering period food such as meat loaf sandwiches and malted milk shakes. Parents and their children dine to piped-in oldies, within an atmosphere resembling that of the *Happy Days* television program.

Rock 'n' roll nostalgia is interesting because of the types of music chosen by programmers to attract and please their audiences. The music is typically 1950s style rockabilly or early 1960s pop rock (e.g., the Beach Boys and Motown groups). The primary audience for oldies programming, however, grew up with the somewhat harsher and harder music of the later 1960s (e.g., psychedelia and anti-war music). Most choose to forsake their own music for the easygoing, fun music of their older siblings who grew up in the 1950s. In the language of postmodernism, the oldies culture is a *simulacrum* (cf. Baudrillard 1983). It never existed in its original state as it is now presented to consumers. Again, adults commonly choose to relive the child-like side of their reconstructed adolescence, not the adult side.

Second, adults may engage in continuous rock 'n' roll experiences that are constructed in the present. Many adults, especially males, maintain their original interest in rock 'n' roll. They are visible at live concerts of 1960s performers who are still "on the road" (e.g., the Rolling Stones, Led Zeppelin, the Who, and the Moody Blues). They continue to buy recorded music, but much less than teen-agers do. An intriguing bonding and gift-giving ritual among middle-class and middle-aged adult males is the exchange of tape dubs. One fan will purchase a new recording (preferably on compact disc) and proceed to dub high quality cassette tape copies for distribution to neighbors, co-workers, business associates, and others with similar tastes. Van Morrison fans are a good example of this trend.

Yet, adults are supported in their pursuit of rock 'n' roll by advances in technology and marketing. Adults can listen to their very specific styles of rock 'n' roll, without the commercials intended for young people, through satellite radio. They can also purchase their music of choice from the comfort of their home office via amazon.com and iTunes.

Adults may also use rock 'n' roll as a medium for rebellion. Practical and proven strategies developed during adolescence to enrage parents and other adults are retrieved to use against current opponents, such as wives. We have heard of men who turn up their stereos at home simply to aggravate their wives. In contrast, we have also heard of wives who banish their husbands to the basement or the garage to play their loud music, similar to the shaming banishment of a cigarette-smoking spouse to the backyard.

Adults as Parents

As we have seen, members of all generations use some version of rock 'n' roll music in everyday life. The major argument here, however, is that rock and pop also serve as a bridge across the generations. Rock and pop are shared by children, adolescents and adults. As one would easily guess, much of this sharing takes place within the family. Yet, contrary to common wisdom, we will argue that much of this sharing is functional and positive: rock and pop help integrate families.

From the early days of Elvis Presley to current issues surrounding rap music, our mass culture has portrayed rock and pop as a source of tension within families (Martin and Segrave 1988). Whether this conflict is over lyrics or volume or whatever, the fact is that children could not experience music without the implicit if not explicit support of their parents (as we have seen in the case of *American Bandstand* and Metallica). The cultural pervasiveness of pop music lets it function in many different ways in the family, much like religion or television have. We will now present an inventory of these—largely taken-for-granted—positive features of pop and rock music.

Mother and Daughter Bonding

Rock and pop have always served as a special commonality between mothers and daughters. They shared Elvis Presley in the 1950s, Frankie Avalon and the Beatles in the 1960s, and Neil Diamond in the 1970s. In the feminist era of the 1980s and 1990s, however, the object of sharing shifted to other women. Madonna is the case in point.

Madonna represents a popular phenomenon that is attractive to both mothers and daughters. Madonna is a multi-faceted star whose appeal rests upon lifestyle, clothing style, and attitude as well as musical performance. During the Houston stop on the "Like a Virgin" tour, Joe interviewed a number of mother-daughter pairs who attended. The pairs typically were dressed alike, in outfits such as black bustier and short black skirts, with matching jewelry. During the interviews, they talked about Madonna in similar ways and appeared more like friends than family. In virtually all cases, they noted a distinct lack of true appreciation of Madonna by the men in their lives (e.g., fathers, husbands, brothers and boyfriends who may look at Madonna and only see a sex object). And in most cases, the mothers indicated that Madonna served to bring them closer to their daughters.

Gwen Stefani is a pop music phenomenon that is attractive to both mothers and daughters. She is an intriguing singer who makes a fashion statement with an attitude. She is one young, but not too young, performer to whom mothers can relate—unlike marginal artists such as Miley Cyrus (to the super young side) or Amy Winehouse (to the edge). Molly is a 45-year-old account executive who accompanied her 17-year-old daughter to a recent Gwen Stefani concert: "I like Gwen Stefani because she reminds me a lot of a younger Madonna. She sings with style and dresses with style—although I would never wear some of her outfits." A currently fashionable style of music shared by mothers and daughters are hip hop performers like Justin Timberlake and Kanye West. Other female pop performers who fit this category include the recent winners of the *American Idol* television competition, Kelly Clarkson and Carrie Underwood.

Father and Son Bonding

Fathers and sons also use rock and pop music to bond, but in different ways than one might expect. Fathers who learned to play guitar in the 1960s or 1970s teach their sons how to play. Sharing music is difficult, as the younger generation today continues the traditional ideological belief that their music is better than that of their parents. Fathers and sons are considerably more vehement than women in their allegiance to their generation's music. In recent years, musical bonding has been relatively easy in light of the resurgence of 1970s and 1980s reunion bands on tour. In 2007 alone, the Rolling Stones, The Police, the Eagles, Led Zeppelin, Bruce Springsteen and the E Street Band, Van Halen, and the Smashing Pumpkins all played the type of loud, guitar-driven rock 'n' roll that many dads and sons can share. Also think of how music-centered video games like Guitar Hero bring together kids and parents to rock out over classic and more recent rock anthems.

During Joe's study of the evolving rave phenomenon in Houston (Kotarba 1993), he heard one 16-year-old boy exclaim: "I hate my dad's music. He listens to that old shit, like Led Zeppelin." On the other hand, recent trends like rave (i.e., dance parties held in clandestine locations, to the beat of loud synthesized music.) display a renaissance in the 1960s counterculture. Psychedelia is "in," for example, with LSD as the drug of choice and lighting provided by mood lamps. Teenagers see rave as a way of retrieving the romance and simplicity of the 1960s. In a way, these kids accept their parents' claim that growing up in the 1960s was special. Another example is Deadhead fathers and their sons sharing the Grateful Dead experience.

In Joe's own family, he had a very special rock 'n' roll experience with his eldest son, when he was five years old. They were driving out to a fishing hole in their old pickup truck, when the local hard rock radio station began playing songs from the Van Halen album "1984." This is one of Joe's all-time favorite albums and, in a sociological sense, definitive of the state of rock music in the mid-1980s. When the pounding, driving anthem "Panama" came on the radio, it began with the loud rumble of a motorcycle taking off. Chris proceeded to jump around in his seat to the excitement of what he knew as the "motorcycle song." Like any proud baby boomer father, a tear left Joe's eye when he realized that his son was OK . . . he liked rock 'n' roll!

Family Leisure Activities

Rock 'n' roll fits well with the burgeoning family leisure and vacation industry. Family theme parks typically have some attraction related to rock 'n' roll, such as the complete mock-up of a 1950s small town main street in the Fiesta Texas theme park in San Antonio. The artists performing at the amphitheaters in the Six Flags parks include REO Speedwagon, the Eagles reunion band, and the latest version of the Jefferson Airplane/Starship.

Whereas the concept "family entertainment" in the 1950s, 1960s, and 1970s referred to phenomena such as wholesome television programming, Walt Disney films and home games, it increasingly refers to pop today. The rock and pop presented usually addresses a common denominator acceptable to both parents and children, such as rockabilly or 1970s power pop groups like Cheap Trick and Aerosmith.

Religious Socialization

Rock 'n' roll functions as a mechanism for teaching religious beliefs and values in families, whether or not rock 'n' roll is compatible with the particular family's religious orientation. For mainstream Protestant denominations, rock 'n' roll increasingly fits the liturgy. For example, when Amy Grant played a concert in Houston several years back as part of her *Angels* album tour, her music was loud and fast (e.g., seven-piece band with double drummers and double lead guitars). Parents accompanying their children to the concert peppered the audience.

One father, in his thirties, brought his wife and 10-year-old daughter to the concert (which he learned about at his Lutheran church). When Joe asked him about the compatibility of Christian rock music with Christianity, he stated:

> We love Amy Grant. She is married and tours with her husband, which is not the case with regular rock stars. Her songs are full of Christian messages. Any way you can get the message of Christ to your kids is OK with us.

The variety of Christian rock styles is growing. A particularly intriguing version is Christian heavy metal (Kotarba 1991). One rock club in Houston routinely books Christian heavy metal bands on Sunday evenings. One evening, they booked a Christian speed metal band, White Cross, that played extremely loud and fast music about Christ. Joe talked to several parents who accompanied their children to the concert. The parents were very polite, clean cut, middle-class, Southern Baptists surrounded by a sea of punk rockers and headbangers. They very much seemed like the parents of the *American Bandstand* generation discussed above. They created the opportunity for their teenagers to attend the concert by carpooling them and their friends in from the suburbs. They hoped that the message emanating from the long-haired rockers was indeed Christian, but they wanted to see for themselves to make sure that Satan was not infiltrating the event.

Certain Christian denominations view rock 'n' roll of any kind as evil, whether under the guise of Christian rock or not. Parents in this faith focus their attention on rock 'n' roll as a way of establishing moral boundaries for their children. For example, a very popular video among conservative youth ministers is called "Rock 'n' roll: A Search for God." The producer, Eric Holmberg, displays numerous rock album covers to illustrate his argument that rockers, especially heavy metal rockers, advertently or inadvertently proclaim satanic messages. For fundamentalist parents, rock 'n' roll functions as a convenient and accessible way of teaching their children clearly and directly that Satan and evil are present in today's world and can take various attractive forms.

Moral Socialization

Rock 'n' roll functions as a mechanism for articulating general moral rules and values for particular groups. Although the PMRC is broadly based politically, it supports the religious right's concern for the threat rock 'n' roll poses to the moral, physical and psychological health of their children (Weinstein 1991). For middle-class and upwardly mobile

African-American parents, rap music clarifies the issue of gender abuse within their community (cf. Light 1992). In a more institutionalized sense, rap music is becoming the medium of choice among inner-city teachers for transmitting emerging moral messages. For example, rap music is now allowed in the Houston public schools for student talent shows. The local news regularly highlights school programs in which students use rap idioms to convey anti-smoking and anti-drug messages.

Historical Socialization

Families use rock 'n' roll to relay a sense of history to their children. For example, every year on Memorial Day in Houston, various veterans' organizations sponsor a concert and rally at the Miller Outdoor Theater. Most of the veterans present fought in Vietnam, the first war for which rock 'n' roll served as the musical soundtrack. Most of the veterans bring their children to the event. Among all the messages and information available to the kids is the type of music popular during the war. A popular band regularly invited to perform is the Guess Who, whose "American Woman" was a major anthem among soldiers. Joe has observed fathers explaining the song to their teen-aged and preteen-aged children, who would otherwise view it as just another of dad's old songs (see Chapter 6).

The current "green" environmental movement is a current illustration of moral socialization. The audience for "Live Earth" in 2007 was very intergenerational and, ironically, created a situation in which children may have sent environmental messages to parents.

CONCLUSION

We have only touched upon the many ways popular music in general and rock 'n' roll specifically works positively for people, as a medium of culture and means to family integration. There are obvious limitations to this analysis. The illustrations certainly do not represent all rock 'n' roll experiences in a systematically sampled way. The generalizations presented here are clearly based primarily upon the experiences of white, middle-class rock 'n' roll fans and their families, yet the principles of family culture use discussed here apply across subpopulations in western societies.

While our empirical focus has been on the family, we have also touched on another important domain of sociological investigation: the study of social problems. The intellectual field of social problems study is predicated on the assumption that social phenomena can be denoted as "problems" because they somehow differ from the norm, the reasonably expected, or simply other phenomena. But when a phenomenon is pervasive throughout or endemic to a group, it is difficult to call it a problem. Rock and pop music are a social problem only if one assumes that it is limited to a portion of the population (teenagers) who use it to harm themselves or others. However, rock and pop "belong" to all portions of the population.

These findings are evidence for the argument that the true "cause" of social problems associated with children and adolescents lie beyond the music they choose to listen to. On the one hand, music simply serves too many positive, integrative functions at the family and individual level for it audiences to be considered a "problem" in its own right. On the other hand, these findings strongly suggest that we look deeper for the roots of children's and adolescents' problems, such as the structure of the family itself. Rock 'n' roll is all too often merely a convenient scapegoat for these problems.

2

DEVIANCE

Deviance—or deviant behavior—has been a topic of interest in modern sociology ever since its inception during the industrial revolution. The study of deviance is crucial to the overall goal of sociology for one simple reason: sociologists believe that social life is closely related to social rules. Some sociologists (e.g., structuralists and functionalists) believe that social rules (e.g., customs, culture, or laws) determine people's behavior, whereas other sociologists (e.g., symbolic interactionists, constructionists) believe that people actively create, negotiate, re-shape, and use social rules to make sense of the situation around them or their own behavior. But regardless of theoretical orientation, deviance is a key lens to a better understanding of social rules, order, and individual and collective behavior.

A simple understanding of deviance conceptualizes the deviant act as deviation from the norm. Basically, for example, if nine people out of ten like melodic music, and one person dislikes melodic music, then that tenth person may be seen as making a deviant musical choice. This conceptualization, however, explains little. Given our analytical approach to social things of all sorts, we prefer to focus on how normal—or non-deviant behavior—is accomplished. This constructionist approach to deviance, and normality, seems to us much better equipped for understanding the meanings shaped by social actors in concert with one another and associated with a sense of order. In order to do this it seems obvious that one of the best—if not the best—ways of studying social rules and order is to observe situations in which the rules are challenged . . . orderly!

All of this can be confusing, so let us proceed slowly. We read in the first chapter about questionable claims that certain styles of popular music, specifically some rock traditions and rap, may "cause" deviance (e.g., suicide or delinquency) among young people. We explained that as an instance of social problem work. In this chapter, we will examine the relationship of pop music to a particular form of deviant behavior (and social problem): illegal drug use. We will not, however, argue that one causes the other. Instead, we will look at the ways designer-drug users make use of internet sites to help them make sense of their behavior, habits, risks, and order their experiences. In other words, in typical interactionist style we want to focus on how social actors define an act as non-deviant within the context of their group culture. This examination is based upon a recent study of one particular internet site (Kotarba 2007).

Musicians, critics, journalists, and fans have long noted the close relationship between popular music and illegal drug use. Some observers frame this relationship negatively, for example, as a path of self-destruction for otherwise talented artists and fans. David Crosby, a member of the rock band Crosby, Stills, and Nash, for example, wrote a very popular autobiography describing the accumulating and debilitating legal and artistic problems in his life attributed to twenty-five years of playing rock and roll while under the influence of abusive amounts of marijuana, heroin, and cocaine (Crosby and Gottlieb 1988). Other observers have focused on the positive aspects of this relationship, for example, the creative impact drug use has had on musical composition, performance and consumption. In their sympathetic biography of Jim Morrison, Jerry Hopkins, and Danny Sugarman (1980: 18) compared the late leader of the Doors to other, self-destructive yet creative poets:

> The romantic notion of poetry was taking hold: the "Rimbaud legend," the destined tragedy, were impressed on his consciousness; the alcoholism of Baudelaire, Dylan Thomas, Brendan Behan; the madness and addiction of so many more in whom the pain married with the visions. . . . To be a poet entailed more than writing poems.

In either case, members of the world of popular music have developed a culture that has provided a rich and complex discursive tradition through which they talk, disseminate information, and share experiences about this relationship. The nature of this discourse has taken different forms over the years as styles of illegal drug use, the objectives of drug talk, and the media by which this talk takes place have all evolved. We refer to this discourse as *drugmusictalk*. This discourse works as a *technique of neutralization*: a practical strategy by which social agents neutralize values which would label their acts as immoral, inappropriate, delinquent, and so forth. A technique of neutralization—a concept coined by Matza and Sykes (1964)—allows a group to go on with their business without feeling shame or guilt. It is a mechanism which allows a belief—such as the conviction that one is doing something wrong—to be suspended. Utilizing this concept should allow us to view the following data not as an example of moral corruption, but instead as an instance of faithful allegiance to group-contingent moral obligations.

We will describe the working of illegal drug talk involving music that takes place on the internet. The case in question is *drugmusictalk* that takes place on one particular internet site dedicated to education for and discussion of responsible drug use, especially designer drugs (e.g., MDMA). Thus, the *drugmusictalk* that takes place on this site provides us with a glimpse into the world of club or designer drugs, rave parties, dance and high technology—and thus into a unique group's counter-culture. As we will show, music is a key feature of this world. We will begin with a quick summary of the history of the relationship of popular music and illegal drug use, followed by a brief discussion of the evolution of *drugmusictalk*. We will then describe the larger project from which the present analysis is derived. We will then present an illustrated inventory of the ways music enters interaction on the internet.

UNDERSTANDING LABELING AND CULTURES OF DEVIANCE: THE RELATIONSHIP OF POPULAR MUSIC AND ILLEGAL DRUG USE

Journalists, scientists, and religious leaders alike have noted the parallel emergence of popular music styles and styles of illegal drug use since the early twentieth century. Obviously, the mixing of drugs (illegal or otherwise) and music occurred much earlier than the twentieth century. This is not to say that all musicians and their audience members use drugs. The point is that these two behaviors combine into lifestyles that, at various times, are seen to be morally, legally, aesthetically, and/or medically problematic. A way to understand this social phenomenon is by referring to how deviant counter-cultures are constructed by both members and by outsiders to the group. Let us begin with outsiders to the group.

In the first chapter we have seen how certain groups of people—moral entrepreneurs—embark in missions to define what is appropriate and what is not. Becker (1963) views the work of moral entrepreneurs as a *crusade* of sorts. As he tells us:

> The crusader is not only interested in seeing to it that other people do what he thinks right. He believes that if they do what is right it will be good for them. Or he may feel that his reform will prevent certain kinds of exploitation of one person by another.
>
> (ibid.: 148)

Sociologically speaking, if a crusade is successful it will result not only in the construction of a social norm, but also in the labeling of those who break it as deviants. *Labeling* is a very important concept. When we label someone as deviant, we exercise a great deal of moral force upon them. As Becker put it, by labeling people we make outsiders of them. Deviance, for Becker and other interactionists, is thus a "consequence of the application by others of rules and sanctions to an 'offender.' The deviant is one to whom the label has been successfully applied" (ibid.: 9).

In his influential study of outsiders, Becker focuses on both the construction and application of social norms, and the consequences of labeling in terms of the identities and social status of those who are labeled. At the time of its publication, and still to this day, Becker's study was revolutionary. Instead of focusing on the structural consequences of objectively defined deviant acts, or instead of treating deviants as pathologically abnormal, Becker posited deviance as an outcome of social interaction. Social norms, in Becker's view, are thus only one of many symbolic and material resources that individuals take into consideration—more or less consciously—when acting in concert with others. Indeed, most social agents are explicitly aware of the importance of social norms. Yet, in some cases, they may put those norms in brackets, build their own norms, and socialize new members to break society-wide rules but faithfully respect group-wide ones instead. The case of certain music cultures seems a perfect example of this.

Take, for instance, blues music. Blues music is one of the earliest styles of distinctively American popular music. The blues emerged in the rural U.S. South and river towns in the 1910s and 1920s (Jones 1963). Although not the exclusive drug of choice among blues performers and their fans, marijuana has been central to the blues scene over the years.

Jazz, on the other hand, emerged at more or less the same time as the blues, but in different locations (e.g., New Orleans and New York) and in a different style of scene (i.e., middle-class African Americans and Caucasians in a very urban setting). Heroin has traditionally been the drug of choice in the jazz world (Jones 1963: 201–202). Jack Kerouak, Allen Ginsburg and other Beat Poets of the 1950s and early 1960s emulated Charley Parker, John Coltrane and other jazz artists' hard lifestyles as well as their work (e.g., Kerouak 1957). The afore-mentioned Howard Becker was himself a jazz musician, and several of his works detail the various deviant behaviors of jazz musicians.

As we move into the 1960s, the presence of recreational drugs became widespread among white adolescents creating and appreciating rock music. Marijuana, alcohol, methamphetamines, and LSD were all very popular, as were the Rolling Stones, Led Zeppelin, and the Beatles. As Lenson (1998) notes, drug use was central to the rock music scene of the late 1960s because it enhanced the experience of improvisation—the hallmark of countercultural music—for both artist and audience. Rock groups today that play this style are commonly known as "jam bands" (e.g., Dave Matthews Band, the Grateful Dead, and The Allman Brothers Band).

The 1970s witnessed a decline in the countercultural power of rock music, within the context of an increasingly conservative, post-Vietnam War society. Instead, we witness the emergence of disco music. The French model of the chic dance nightclub arrived almost intact in New York in the early 1960s. This model became the scene for the drug-fueled cultural revolution of that era. Popularly known as "disco" in the 1970s, the phenomenon confronted white, heterosexual America with the newly liberated gay lifestyle, which was dedicated to rampant prom-iscuity and avid, recreational drug use (Braunstein 1999). Popular drugs in the disco scene included amphetamines, methamphetamines, and marijuana.

The 1970s and 1980s marked the advent of punk and heavy metal music. To some degree, both styles of music involved a return to injected drugs among marginal segments of their respective scenes. Pills of various kinds were popular as well as traditional marijuana. The wholesale movement of illegal drug use emerged out of the black community and into white suburbia. Punk and heavy metal elicited great response from agents of social control—for example, Tipper Gore's Parents Music Resource Center—who saw the link between these styles of music and drug use as a major social problem (Krauss 1991).

The emergence of rap music as a feature of the broader hip hop culture in the late 1980s was marked by accusations of its links with growing crack cocaine use. Freebasing became popular in the 1980s among the poor because it was an economical way for them to enjoy cocaine—ironically, a vice for the privileged classes in earlier years. Beginning with Grandmaster Flash and the Furious Five's "White Lines," crack cocaine became a central theme in rap music (George 1998).

The popular music scene at the turn of the century witnesses a major turn to techno music, dance, and designer drugs. Specifically, the literature on techno dance and drugs gives one the impression that the increase in the use of ecstasy (MDMA) and the growth of the Technoscene, especially in the 1990s, are highly correlated. Hitzler (2002) notes that most ecstasy users in Europe identify themselves as fans of techno/rave, and those techno fans who consume drugs generally prefer ecstasy.

So, what exactly is going on with these musical subcultures and countercultures? Why is it that a deadhead is praised by her peers for smoking marijuana but chastised for doing speed? Or why is that a rave fan chooses designer drugs but strongly rejects others? While there are many possible reasons—and sociological literature is available on a variety of these—let us focus on issues of deviance and identity. According to interactionists, labeling most often results in the generation of *self-fulfilling prophecies*. A self-fulfilling prophecy is the realization of a possibility. It works like this: (1) moral entrepreneurs engage in work over the definition of a particular situation, act, or value as deviant and in the consequent labeling of those who break thus defined rules; (2) rule-breakers are treated as such by various rule-enforcement agents: as outsiders, pathological individuals, criminals, problem-ridden deviants; (3) rule-breakers internalize the notion that they are indeed different than the norm; and finally (4) rule-breakers, who now identify themselves as such, will act in deviant ways. The rule breakers are thus "made" in social interaction. And while at times they may staunchly resist their labeling, at other times they will enjoy their deviant identity as a badge of honor. Becker writes (1963: 2–3):

> The person who is thus labeled an outsider may have a different view of the matter. He may not accept the rule by which he is being judged and may not regard those who judge him as either competent or legitimately entitled to do so. Hence, a second meaning of the term emerges: the rule-breaker may feel his judges are outsiders.

What Becker describes is a technique of neutralization: a technique by which the jazz cat who does dope is cool, and the outsider nothing but a square.

So, in summary, drugs and popular music often go together. Attempting to establish a causal link working like a hypodermic needle injecting deviant ideas into people's minds would be an oversimplification. Fans not only emulate musicians' work, but also emulate their lifestyles because they may share the same cultural values, conventions, and practices. Fans—and critics—see drugs (and not all of them, but particular ones different from scene to scene) as central to the music, creativity, and overall social world of the musician.

MUSIC AND DRUG DISCOURSE

The popular music scenes mentioned above have all contained a way of communicating about music and drugs. This communication generally reflects current musical fashion; drug fashion; and available as well as desirable communication media. Traditionally, members of a scene are likely to engage in *drugmusictalk* for the following purposes (among others):

- to share aesthetic drug-music experiences;
- to discuss fit between particular drugs and styles of music;
- to share affective aspects (e.g., sexuality) of drug-music experiences;
- to discuss economic and/or ideological aspects of drug-music experiences;
- to discuss personal tastes in music.

Blues music, for example, emerged as a true form of folk music. The distinction between performers and audience members was often blurred, as everyone might take turns singing, playing and listening to stories relevant to the everyday lives of all present. Repression from slavery at first and sheer racism later resulted in the need for blues musicians and their audiences to disguise the potentially radical messages in the music. Much of the *drugmusictalk* was encoded in the lyrics of the blues singers' songs in metaphors and innuendo. In addition, the lack of financial resources among blues people precluded any attempt at developing an organized press to disseminate information about the blues (Jones 1963).

The jazz community, oriented around a largely instrumental style of music, developed *drugmusictalk* in the actual conversation between and among musicians, audience members, and others. The jazz world's version of *drugmusictalk* was created by both the heroin addict and the musician together: As Leroy Jones observes:

> much of the "hip talk" comes directly from the addicts jargon as well as from the musician's. The "secret" bopper's and (later) hipster's language was the essential part of a cult of redefinition, in terms closest to the initiated.
>
> (1963: 202)

Since jazz became a widely recorded style of music, marketed in entertainment centers like New York City, it produced a new form of *drugmusictalk* known as jazz music criticism. Newspaper writers and magazines dedicated to jazz (e.g., Down Beat) conveyed the jazz vernacular to a wide and appreciative audience.

The development of rock music in the late 1960s was marked very clearly by an appropriation of African-American music and drug behavior by white adolescents (Frith 1981: 192). *Drugmusictalk* was imbedded in lyrics of many songs (e.g., "White Rabbit" by the Jefferson Airplane among many others). As Market (2001) observes:

> Songs dealing with illegal drugs have long dotted popular music. It was not until the aftermath of the sixties youth counterculture, however, that drug lyrics became a recurring musical motif. In the decades since, the lyrical treatment of drugs has undergone change. Heroin and cocaine have largely, though not exclusively, been treated antagonistically, with the animosity toward cocaine becoming more pronounced after crack cocaine was introduced in the mid-1980s. Marijuana, on the other hand, has generally been perceived as innocuous, if not positively assessed, and this treatment has crossed the decades into the nineties. In more recent years, however, the positive assessment of marijuana has undergone change, with younger musicians more likely to decry the harm that drugs do than older musicians do. This prosocial aspect of contemporary popular music has been largely ignored.

Nevertheless, the counterculture was also notable for developing its own media, in the form of *Rolling Stone Magazine*, FM radio, concert fliers, and community-based, underground newspapers and journals (Market 2001). Later versions of rock music, specifically heavy metal, developed a multi-media and diverse system of *drugmusictalk*. Pareles (1988) uses the early career of popular heavy metal band Metallica to illustrate this point:

> The heavy metal rock band Metallica plays loud, high-speed music with lyrics that dwell on dark subjects such as death, madness, nuclear war, and drug abuse. While adhering to heavy metal's basic tenets, the members of Metallica rebel against many of the conventions associated with hard rock music and refuse to package themselves for mass consumption. The band has never made a video for MTV, and, until the advent of all-hard-rock radio formats, Metallica albums were never played on commercial rock radio stations. Nonetheless, the group has attracted an avid following, mainly through tours, heavy metal fan publications, some college radio exposure, and word of

mouth. With its skittish, hard-driving music, Metallica manages to avoid the formulaic quality of most heavy metal bands.

Interestingly, agencies of social control, such as the American Medical Association, interpret the lyrics in heavy metal music as dangerous to its fans:

> The American Medical Association (AMA) and the American Academy of Pediatrics have voiced concerns about certain lyrics used in heavy metal and rap music. The AMA says that messages in these genres may pose a threat to the physical health and emotional well being of particularly vulnerable children and adolescents. The AMA has identified six potentially dangerous music themes: drug and alcohol abuse, suicide, violence, satanic worship, sexual exploitation, and racism. Both the AMA and the Academy of Pediatrics support voluntary regulation and increased social responsibility in the music industry.
>
> (Levine 1991)

The next, major development in *drugmusictalk* was the vernacular that emerged from the rap and hip hop culture. Recall that the *drugmusictalk* that accompanied the blues and jazz was intended to keep the larger, often judgmental, white world out of the scene. Rap and hip hop talk shoved the everyday life world of Compton CA, Brooklyn NY, and Houston TX right in the face of anyone willing to listen—whites included.

The most recent style of *drugmusictalk* is the communications taking place in the world of rave parties, techno dance clubs, and designer drugs—the focus of the present discussion. Communications in the early days of rave/techno were fairly primitive—artistic party fliers, dance floor talk, and telephone (Collin 1997). Eventually, rave entrepreneurs developed fan magazines dedicated to rave/techno, as well as the most dramatic development of all: the widespread use of the internet among rave/techno participants (Cummings 1994).

STUDYING *DRUGMUSICTALK*

If we choose to understand reality from the perspective of those whom we wish to study, we need to adopt research methods that allow us to define things as our "research subjects" do. *Inductive* research methods are such tools. An inductive method is a method that allows us to keep a mind as open as possible. An inductive research design is a design that begins not with a hypothesis but with a broad open-ended question that allows us to gather rich, nuanced, descriptive data. The inductive study that Joe conducted on *drugmusictalk* examined the internet as a social scene in its own right, and not just as a means of communicating. His study was part of a larger, team project that included researchers from Texas A&M University as well as the University of Houston (Murguia *et al.* 2007). The primary research question in fancy words was: What is the structure and function of *drugmusictalk* in the context of the internet? In order to answer this question, Joe needed an inductive instrument, if you will, a window for *seeing* specific words and behaviors on the internet sociologically. We call the window a *theoretical framework*. The theoretical framework for this study is symbolic interactionism, as it is for most of the ideas expressed in this book. Just to refresh our idea, in general symbolic interactionism argues that social life is constructed through various forms of interaction. People interact with each other to pragmatically arrive at solutions for shared problems, most often experienced in concrete situations.

Rather than hypotheses, variables, and law-like statements, symbolic interactionists make use of *sensitizing concepts*: concepts which—like tools ready to work in multiple settings—allow for understanding and description. Altheide (2001), an interactionist, discusses one of these concepts: the idea of *media logic*. This concept tells us that the format and the conventions of a medium, in this case the internet, largely shape the structure and function of discourse that occurs in that medium. Contemporary media, especially the internet, empower speakers to create realities (Denzin 1997). Thus media are more than just the message: they are the shape of the world in which lives are lived and cultures are constructed. As Joe has argued earlier, the media logic of the internet specifically allows people to recreate the self situationally and constantly (Kotarba 2002b). A symbolic interaction window sees the internet as if it were any other "real-life" setting studied by sociologists. The medium has evolved and the vernacular has changed, but we can expect many of the same pressing, everyday issues to be at the heart of electronic communication.

There are two sources of data for this analysis. The first is a content analysis of one particular internet site's forums. The following are the forums in which music and drug topics are discussed:

- *Music & DJs*
- Words
- Drug Culture
- Good Experiences
- Bad Experiences.

Research team members searched for elements of *drugmusictalk* and categorized them inductively, following the logic of *grounded theory*.

Grounded theory is a style of social scientific analysis that operates with the logic of induction. Patterns emerge from a constant comparison of cases continuously chosen to seek variation. When variation is exhausted, findings are organized into categories, which themselves are exhausted (Charmaz 2000). In the present study, the essential research question is: what are the various ways participants in the internet site discuss music and drugs? Finally, we analyzed the responses to three items included in the Texas A & M University Survey 2002 on club drugs on the internet (Murguia *et al.* 2007).

TRADITIONAL *DRUGMUSICTALK* THEMES

The participants to the internet site talk about the five traditional *drugmusictalk* topics listed above. We will present examples of each theme. The reader should keep in mind that these themes typically overlap in actual posts. Any one post can contain more than one theme.

Sharing Aesthetic Drug-Music Experiences

The internet site participants talk about their drug music experiences as if they were artistic or theatrical performances. This discourse is frequently sprinkled with efforts to describe the sublime pleasures associated with dancing. The stories tend to be long, well-written narratives. For example:

> Alright, for some background information . . . I have taken a fair amount of pills in my pill career, the most taken in a night being 3 and the most taken at one time being 1. I have never double dropped because I'm too worried about the tolerance that it might develop for future rolls. I usually have a relatively high tolerance to mdma, one pill not taking me as high as most but I don't usually chase highs. I prefer to take pills to enhance the music and the dancing when I go out. I usually start off on a whole then take halves to keep the peak up until I start the downward spiral.
>
> Oher drugs I've had are weed, speed, rush (amyl), acid and dxm. The pills I had were white MX's, very clean strong mdma if you haven't heard of them.
>
> 11pm—Arrived at a one of my preferred nightclubs for an uplifting trance night with a few friends and was gobsmacked by the production of the club-night, starting off an awesome night. Sat around and started to feel the music and dance in my seat, already mystified by the lasers on the dancefloor.

11:30pm—Shafted my first pill. It had to be one of the most uncomfortable things I have ever done to myself and the only thing that pushed me knuckle past knuckle was the thought of a pill high like never before. Apart from the sensation of a finger briefly being up my exit hole, it felt okay and bearable. If anything there was a weird feeling like in 20 minutes I would need to go to the toilet but I knew it was just the pill dissolving. I sat back down and got into the mood of the night. One friend had shafted a whole and another had shafted a half and swallowed the other. I knew what to expect of these pills so I played the waiting game, eager to see what an 80–90% absorption rate from different mdma receptors would be like.

12:00am—One of my favourite DJ's was going to start in half and hour and the dance floor hadn't fully packed out yet so we went up to dance. As soon as I stood up I thought "oooooh I feel good!" There was a feeling of warmth going all over my body but it felt like it was coming from my lower abdomen or even inside my ass! Probably quite true. Starting dancing and getting into the music forgetting about the pill but already feeling great. . . .

I hope you got something from my report ☺ Thanks for reading if you got this far.

Music plays a key role in this type of adventure. It provides something to do, as well as a context for other things to do. Music also functions as something to talk about, as well as something to use to display one's skill, at evaluating and critiquing key features of the techno and dance lifestyle, such as drugs. Drugs, as this case exemplifies, are not always consumed "with success." As Becker (1963) wrote, part and parcel of the process of becoming an outsider—a deviant—has to do with *learning the ropes* of a group a culture. *Learning to enjoy the effects* of rule-breaking—such as drug-consumption—is one of the most central aspects of the process of socialization to a culture of deviance (and one of the most remarkable insights of Becker's inductive analysis).

Discussing the Fit between Particular Drugs and Styles of Music

As we said earlier, there is a definite correspondence between a particular culture of deviance and their internal rules. Popular music scholar Richard Middleton (1990: 9) calls this correspondence an instance of *homology:* "a structural resonance . . . between the different elements making up a socio-cultural whole." Internet site participants display several instances of homology by talking about the fit between drugs and music much like a chef designs a menu—and, the menu can be very long! The following postings illustrate the holistic nature of designer drug experiences:

> as everyone knows music is awsome as hell on E . . . but what music should i download to listen to when im rollin? can neone give me some songs?

and the following answers

> listen up. it all depends on wut u like when you are sober. Xtc will make it sound 10X better. do a search for what kidn of music do you like to listen to when rolling. I have a funny feeling this is gunna get shutdown or booted off to music forum.

and

> love to start off listening to a little rap when i am comin up, then when i start peaking i love to listen to techno. . . . try somethin like darude—sandstorm for some old school stuff, or maybe if u like the radio stuff, dj sammy we're in heaven (but i dont recommend it) i looooove to listen to zombie nation—oh oh oh oh oh . . . and on the comedown some pink floyd suits me, even though it is kinda depressing. so thats me, i dono about u.

and

> that isn't techno, its electronica, but more specificly cheese-trance and i probably wouldn't even call that commercial shit electronica.
> for me, trance/hard-trance is fkn awesome while peaking coz trance takes you on a journey ☺but it might not be for u, but id recommend giving it a try.
> try these: Plastic Boy—Live Another Life (Original Mix)
> Rank 1—Sensation 2003 Anthem
> nu nrg- butterfly
> Angelic—Can't Keep Me Silent (Dumonde Mix)
> BK—Revolution
> Cj Bolland—The Prophet (Original Mix)
> dave 202 and phil green—legends (club mix)
> DJ Air—Alone With Me (Flutlicht Mix)
> DJ Wag—The Darkness
> Green Court—Silent Heart (Flutlicht Remix)
> Kamaya Painters- Far From Over
> Haak—Frenzy
> frank trax—nebuchan (organ remix)
> matanka—lost in a dream (push remix)

Push—Till We Meet Again
Signum—Coming on Strong (SHOKK remix)
Andy B Jones—In Motion (Arrowhead Mix)
Dave 2002—The Klammt (Evacuation Remix)
The Mystery—Devotion (Tatana Remix)
NRC—Here Comes The Rain (Push Remix)
Shane 54—Vampire
DJ Tatana—Moments (flutlicht remix)
Signum—Cosmos
The Gift—Love Angel (M.I.K.E. mix). . . .

and

for rolling and dancing: hard house, progressive and techno
for rolling, chilling and enjoying the music: trance or psy trance
because it makes me trip in a beautiful way. hip hop suits me a
lot better when stoned, when rolling I need stuff on 120–140
BPM, but electronica in general (stuff like Orbital or FSOL is
amazing on E).

These musical and drug suggestions are interesting because they
include only the names for musical performers and performances. The
poster assumes that the respondent is a member already socialized into
the group culture who therefore understands what the terms mean and
who the suggested artists are. These assumptions mark some of the
essential criteria for sheer membership in the subculture.

Indeed, one of the more interesting findings from the data from
items on music and drugs was the style in which internet site participants answered the following question: "What types of music seem to
go best with specific types of drug experiences?" The following is a
brief albeit representative sample of responses. The first type response
is simply and direct. It mirrors the way earlier blues, jazz and rock
audiences largely perceived their drug and music options:

Classical and Rock are by far the best to listen to when high/
drunk.

and

Techno is best with ecstasy.

The second type of response illustrates the essential complexity of the
techno/dance culture that lies beyond mere dichotomous choices:

Smoking cannabis alone at home: any music. I like also otherwise smoking cannabis with friends at home, in a park or other
controllable environment: electronic music with a rich sound

environment (Astral Projection, Hallucinogen). Mushrooms: something peaceful and rich in sounds, as Pink Floyd or Twin Peaks soundtrack. Ecstasy: fast techno music

and

> Although individual preference plays a large part. I think fairly fast slightly hypnotic yet melodic music with anthemic breaks goes down well with most people on most drugs. Generally speaking trance, house, happy hardcore.

The third type of response illustrates a sophisticated mastery of the phenomenon:

> Trance/progressive/techno (not happy hardcore I may add)/hard-house—pills and cannabis. Trance makes you rush like mad, dancing to progressive stuff on pills is wicked and techno just makes a weird underground atmosphere. Hard house is good if you just want to get more off it, bit faster more energetic. Psychedelic Trance—obviously Lsd, shrooms e. t. c All well produced dance music sounds good when stoned.

and

> That is an entirely personal question (greatly varying between people), but for myself I would say that ambient techno (some orbital, Groove Armada) "chick music" (sarah mclachlan, tori amos, etc.) are good for home experiences with one other friend. This makes the experience very calming, less chaotic and quite personal. Industrial techno, jungle, house and happy hardcore techno are lovely for a large gathering of people, say a party or rave. This keeps people active, moving and fluid.

and

> Music parallels the attitude of those drawn to it, and thus the type of feeling desired from the drugs. These are mass generalizations, but from my experience. . . . MDxx—Trance (the uplifting, almost spine tingling nature of the music parallels that of the feeling you get from ecstasy). Amphetamines—Hardcore or Drum n bass (the sped up basslines parallel the sped up nature of the drug). Marijuana—Downtempo (the chilled out nature of the music parallels the chilled out nature of the drug). Alcohol—House (im not quite sure why this works. it just does. Who doesnt like drinking and dancing all night to some disco? i suppose the relaxed funky attitude of the music parallels that of the drug)

The most sophisticated responses seem to come from older (twenties and thirties), college-educated, male participants. They talk about music and drugs in ways very much like older wine connoisseurs talk about which cut of beef goes best with a frisky merlot. Interestingly, most respondents who go into great detail on this item list alcohol and place it very specifically in their inventories. Simpler responses tend to state that alcohol—or marijuana for that matter—go with all sorts of music.

Sharing Affective Aspects (e.g., Sexual) of Drug-Music Experiences

The sexual dimension of drug-music experiences is an important topic for internet site discussions. These stories perhaps illustrate best the social aspects of illegal drug use, as well as the impact on intimate relationships. For example,

> so here's my story, it's a bit long. I'm going through an incredible time in my life, something which happens once in a lifetime. I've done E 2 weeks ago for the last time, it was incredible. I've been doing E for a year now, once every 3 weeks and it's always been great. I'll always remember what happened the first time, it was a life-changing experience. I'll always remember my last time because it was an experience which truly and fully opened my mind to some of the ways of friendship and love I haven't even imagined. I did it with other three people in a Summer Solstice Party in a forest. The after party was at a friend's house. My best friend, and now I know this. And that night was his first pill!!!

> I'm in love with his ex-girlfriend, his most important girlfriend and it seems that she is in love with me. The last time on E he realized that, and he also realized that our love is real, this thing was something that strengthened our friendship in the purest way. I still can't believe that he wants us to be together. Me and her, and me and him. And this morning I realized he even helped the whole thing. Man my last time on E was an incredible journey, maybe I'll do a trip report when I calm down and analyze fully the whole situation.

> Last friday I was at a club with two girls, really close friends, great house tunes, great place, great party . . . I had a pill in my pocket . . . and I didn't eat it!!! I was willing to eat it, a lot. But I didn't. I danced 4 hours in a row just on 2 drinks, it wasn't near as good as on E, but I was happy, so happy that I didn't eat the damn pill, and I was happy in general. The day after I was with her and some other people. She told me a lot of very important things, including she wasn't ever trying ecstasy, she wanted me to tell her

everything about E, but she has decided that she won't do it. She also told me that she didn't mind if I took it in moderation. And she made me understand that she really believes in our relationship which is just starting. I'm 29 but feel like if I was 16, this is the most beautiful thing that has ever happened in my whole life. The night after our conversation, I didn't sleep, I had this pure euphoric feeling, well you know, way beyond what ecstasy could give you, and I even put some tunes on and it was incredible the way I was hearing the music, better than on E.

Tonight I'm taking her for our first real date. And I'm thinking on quitting E. She will even let me go to Ibiza this summer, but I don't see the point anymore. My next pill is due two weeks from now, a big party, the biggest summer party in my town, organized by friends of mine. I'll be taking E for the last time, if I do. I won't be trying convincing her in trying E. She knows what she wants really well, and I think she just wants me, sober and no chemicals. Maybe I won't be reading this board for a while. I love you people. I love E, it really made me the way I am now, and I feel like I'm on top of the world. But I know my next pill won't be that special thing, because there's something alive and real and it's so very special for me right now. Happy rolls and peace and love everybody.

This story illustrates nicely how potential partners negotiate drugs—E, specifically in this case—as a component of their relationship. The relationship itself is constantly evolving, and with it choices for deviant acts change as well. Interactionists like to refer to temporal trajectories of deviant behaviors and attitudes as *moral careers*. A moral career is a career like any other, only it focuses on changing acts, motives, and sentiments that have a strong moral dimension. For example, Davis (2006) has shown how getting married and having kids is an important career contingency within the moral career of a deviant person (indeed, it often ends the deviant habits of many drug-using music fans).

Discussing Economic and/or Ideological Aspects of Drug-Music Experiences

Economic and/or ideological aspects of drug-music experiences are very common in *drugmusictalk*. These are also especially interesting to us because they allow us to understand how members of these groups make sense of their deviant acts. A sensitizing concept which is particularly useful for us in the context is the aforementioned techniques of neutralization. Take the following excerpt from the data, for example, an instance of behavior that seems more typical of largely male members who are a bit older than most, pursue these topics:

> just because you download EDM doesnt mean that you are going to be are worried about being caught then do not share files . . . as soon as you download them move them to another folder that isnt shared. also there is a program out there called peerguard (something like that). from what i understand it uses a list of known RIAA ip addresses and blocks them from connecting to your computer. again, this increases the changes that the RIAA wont catch you, but it does not make you 100% safe. the only way to really be 100% is to stop using p2p/file sharing apps all togeather, but really now, whos gonna do that? think about it thou. how many ppl share files over the net? millions? more? how many people get caught? 1000? less?

By arguing for the high frequency of a deviant act—illegal music downloading—this man is *normalizing* (or in other words deproblematizing) this behavior. The strategy of normalizing is typically used by many drug users too. Think of how many times you have heard the argument that marijuana consumption should be decriminalized because "just about everyone does it, and it's impossible to capture most people anyway!" This technique of neutralization is called a *denial of injury:* a process whereby the offender claims that no one is getting hurt in the process. Other techniques of neutralization include *denials of responsibility, denial of the victim, condemnation of the condemners,* and *appealing to higher loyalties* (Matza and Sykes 1964). By normalizing behavior labeled as deviant, people defend their sense of self from any *stigmatization.* This is why techniques of neutralization are considered a form of *stigma management* (for more on this, see Goffman 1963).

Discussing Personal Tastes in Music

Participants talk about their favorite styles of music. As we have already seen, the many terms used to identify musical styles allow respondents to custom design on-line identities and proclaim their membership in the subculture. The many terms used to identify music styles also index the fragmentation of popular music culture in the postmodern era (Jameson 1991). The following is a partial list of rave music styles:

> DnB; Progressive; Hard Trance; Industrial; Metal; Rock; Classical; Andrew's Sisters (40's group); 80's Love Songs; African tribal music; trance (deeeeeep!); Rock; Classical; electronica; African tribal music; Drum & Bass; Jungle; U.K. Garage; Hip Hop; Hard Trance; NRG Jungle; Breakbeat; Techno; Acid; Jazz; Alternative;

pop; downtempo; breaks; techno; dnb RnB; Reggae; Soul; Small elements of rock, certain tunes that I happen to like . . . Jam Music; Reggae; Jazz; Techno; Old Skool Hip Hop; Deep House; Classic Rock; Ska.

Interestingly, music fans who are not participants in the techno/rave/ dance scene have great difficulty differentiating among these many various styles or subgenres. There are three possible explanations for this complex phenomenon. First, multiple musical styles represent a cultural value in the scene. High status is attached to members who are sophisticated in their taste in music. The ability to differentiate and choose among many subgenres illustrates this sophistication. Second, dance music by itself is pretty simple music; it is rhythm-intensive and repetitive. Dance music lacks the textual complexity of lyrics. Participants in the dance music scene may maintain if not rejuvenate interest in the scene by creating subgenres. Third, and perhaps most relevant to this discussion, outsiders are oblivious to the nuances and variations within dance music because the nuances and variations are only perceivable when high on drugs. Take, as a further example, this post on musical equipment:

> yeah i wanna get some decks, a decent mixer with a beat counter
>   (yeah i know im a shit cunt) and some headphones. im in
>   australia and i was wondering if this equip is ok
> —2x Stanton STR830 direct drive turntables.
> —1x behringer VMX200 mixer
> —unsure about headphones yet.
> this will set me back $1187 for the decks and mixer. what i was
>   wanting to know is this equipment any good for a beginner
>   (i can mix alright) or should i just find something else.
> this stuff is brand new.
> Dfi ☺

The great complexity and sophistication we see in the taxonomy of musical styles known and used by music fans are a mirror reflection of the complexity and sophistication of their understanding of drugs and drug use. Again, they fancy themselves connoisseurs of their lifestyles and their culture, and by displaying their knowledge they strengthen their status within the counterculture. We can refer to this as an instance of *idioculture*: "a system of knowledge, beliefs, behaviors, and customs shared by members of an interacting group to which members can refer and employ as the basis of further interaction" (Fine 1979). Idioculture are typical of many deviant groups, but are also typical of non-deviant groups as well.

The Internet Allows People to Create and
Perform Situational Identities

As we will see in Chapter 6, postmodern existentialism tells us that the contemporary experience of self is complex and situational. We can be different things—to ourselves and to others—as the situation requires and our past experience suggests (Kotarba 2002b). Due to its higher potential for interaction the internet provides a great opportunity to create, develop, and project a self in a way never available to older media. The internet allows for long and immediate, narrative presentations of self. Describing one's self is not constrained by the grammatical and stylistic constraints posed by older media. The great complexity of the site-structure of the internet—with its chat rooms, forums, and homepages—allows a wide variety of venues to write for a very specific and directed audience, an audience as close to one's interests and expertise as ever possible in the history of communications.

Yet, in our mass-mediated, postmodern world, people can be different selves at different time in different situations. Internet site participants may be different self-identities in other aspects of their lives, in front of other audiences. I posted the following question on the "music and drugs" board: "Why do so many people hate country music?" The following are typical responses:

> Good gawd!

> How the f*ck did we get on the topic of country music!? I mean seriously, MAN!!! What's going on!? This is the 21st century! Nobody loses their girlfriend, their dog and their trailer anymore.

> They should update their shit—how about: Blue Screen Of Death Blues

> Dude, just cause you hate contry doesnt mean you gotta knock it to peeps that do. Just say you dont like it. . . . without the "BARF" and shit like that. If your a DJ then you should know the appreciation of music. I dont like country either . . . but i know plenty of peeps that do . . . there is nothing wrong with that. I cant say that i like being in a room of it playing for hours on end . . . but its def not the end of the world. just like someone you know maynot like your music . . . but might just put up with it.

Internet site participants locate their selves directly in their drug experiences. Music makes these selves all the more complex, elegant, desirable, esteemed, and worthwhile. For example:

So the question is: "When you are rolling what gets you in that 'ecstasy' state more: hard pounding energetic music or smoother and gentler music?"

Personally for me its gentler music because when I'm rolling my mind can't really keep up with all the hard pounding intriquet sounds . . . it becomes too chaotic that I get annoyed . . . but when I listen to some smooth gentle trance that progresses very nicely from an ambient beginning to a climatic end I drift away into bliss. Music that is constantly energetic is too much for me, but I *can* handle music that is very energetic but in waves. And I can't stand extremely slow music, like I said before, song has to come in waves of energy or I get bored with it . . . I'm VERY picky while rolling. Oddly enough it is the opposite when I'm sober . . . I love hard pounding insane music that never ceases with it's energy instead of slow builds and dreamy soundscapes. Weird huh? What about you? Hard and Banging or Gentle and Progressive?

and

depends on my point in the roll really, if im coming up or down, something gentle (preferably with some amazing vocals), but if im in the strong part of the roll i prefer some BANGIN hard music so i can dance my ass off).

These statements of course can be understood by referring back to our discussion about the labeling of acts, and people, as deviant, and the relevance of that labeling for the development of identity.

CONCLUSION

Internet sites appear to be a desirable and useful venue for talking about one's music, dance, and drug experiences holistically, as they occur in everyday life. The strength of the internet site as a medium, from the participants' perspectives, is that it provides the opportunity to share these experiences with others very much like them. The liability, from a social control perspective, is that the internet site provides the opportunity to *celebrate* these experiences.

Drugmusictalk describes many different ways music relates to the designer drug experience for internet site participants. They use music to generate a meaning context for their drug experiences. Music functions as a stimulant for drug experiences and an element—an important one—of a group's idioculture. Listening to music provides ways to pass time during drug experiences, and to establish mood during drug experience. Music also has a distinctive social function in a world in which drugs, dancing and other behaviors are very individualistic: it provides something to do together during drug experiences. Finally, music can serve as a depressant for drug experience, to counteract the high associated with rave/techno/designer drugs.

Our analysis of *drugmusictalk* illustrates the great service a sociological approach can provide to the understanding of deviant behavior. Sociologists must avoid trying to explain people's behavior—that is a job for psychologists and biological scientists. Our job is to show as clearly and as precisely as possible, how people work very hard to pull off their activities, whether or not they abide by their rules or the rules of others.

3

THE ECONOMY

Sociologists understand the economy as that social institution which encompasses organization, customs, and practices focused on the global production, distribution, and consumption of goods and services. Contemporary Western economic systems are dependent on market trade of commodities for profit, rather than barter-based or gratuitous exchange. The logic of this system—known as *capitalism*—is strong enough to expand wider and wider to multiple areas of life. Thus, within capitalism many goods and services that have traditionally been exchanged without the mediation of money (like music, to some extent) have now become commodified. An astute commentator from the Frankfurt School of Critical Theory, Walter Benjamin, observed that the commodification of original expressions like art is typical of a society in which the mechanical reproduction of artistic texts and performances is possible. While mechanic reproduction takes away from the "aura" of the original, it makes every copy a product valuable on its own (Benjamin 1969). In turn, the uses and gratifications that people derive from exchanges of the original and its copies have become commodified as well. This process, known as *commodification*, is of great interest to students of both sociology writ large and popular music and will be the object of our attention in this chapter.

Within a post-industrial society, popular music and related commodities are uniquely significant goods and services because their study allows us to understand the logic of capitalism, with its efficiencies and contradictions. *Post-industrialism* is a historical period—the one in which we currently live—characterized by a global manufacturing system based on the utilization of advanced technologies of production, service work, and decentralized and hyperspecialized corporate production. Popular music within this period is characterized by the preponderance of the exchange of sound recordings and related products manufactured through the latest technologies; by the paid work (writing, performance, promotion and, distribution) of a wide variety of professionals (rather than amateurs) working in the tertiary sector of the economy; and by musical production under an enormous multitude of labels dispersed around the globe that are controlled by a small number of multinational corporations. More importantly, post-industrial economies and societies revolve—both in financial and cultural terms—around practices of individual *consumption* for survival and growth. The use of popular music in everyday life within this system is thus best understood as a multifaceted form of symbolic consumption.

In this chapter, we examine the intersection between music and the economy by focusing on three closely interrelated aspects of music consumption and production. We begin with an analysis of the popular music business within the context of teen pop. The genre of teen pop serves as a great example of the *concentration of capital* in the hands of a few corporate actors which control artistic talent, style, and thus to some extent what music audiences will consume. Even more significantly the example of teen pop allows us to understand how musical expression within post-industrial society works by the standards of a capitalistic economy and culture. Subsequently, we shift our attention to a classic sociological concept—dating as far back as the turn of the twentieth century—*conspicuous consumption*. In a case study of the decentralization of musical sound we examine how popular music has become a practice less exclusively revolving around sound and more about image as musical performers and popular media attempt to expand the logic of capitalism in music to many areas of everyday life, especially those related to lifestyle and the presentation of the bodily self and identity. Finally, through a brief consideration of a variety of uses of music in social contexts we examine the extent to which music is used as commercial technology.

OLIGOPOLY AND ITS CONSEQUENCES

Within economics and sociology the concept of *oligopoly* refers to circumstances in which a small number of competing actors have economic control of a particular enterprise. The term is closely related to that of oligarchy—which refers to circumstances in which a small number of actors hold the political control of a society—but has a purely economic denotation. The contemporary popular music industry is marked by an oligopoly of five giant corporations who together control about four-fifths of global music sales. Today the five companies are known as the "Big 5" and include the German BMG, the British EMI, the Japanese Sony, the American WEA (a subsidiary of AOL Time-Warner), and the truly international Universal Music Group. These five major labels are often referred to as "the majors." An enormously vast group of labels called "independents" or "indies" share the rest of global revenues from music. Despite this seemingly sharp division many majors and indies often share resources or do business together. For example, many indies rely on majors for distribution of their repertoire and majors depend on indies to scout and sign emerging talent. Indies are better prepared to develop artistic talent outside of the mainstream genres because of their "street" credibility, keener knowledge of practices and conventions existing within a local scene, and their tendency to give artists more creative freedom—among other reasons. On the other hand, the majors control the Top 40 or "pop" music scene thanks to their ability to coordinate costly multimedia promotion campaigns. Indies and majors also have another important characteristic in common: both depend on the success of a very small group of artists who alone carry the entire franchise on their backs by compensating for the losses or modest profits emanating from other less popular artists. In light of this, having one artist (for indies) or a handful of artists (for majors) ranked in the "Top 40" may mean big business.

As a musical category "Top 40" is hardly a logical, or at least a homogenous one. Merely referring to the fact that a recording has reached the top of the charts, "Top 40" may refer to musical genres as diverse as new age, hardcore punk, heavy metal, dance, and hip pop. Yet, there is a tendency for many "Top 40" songs to resemble one another in terms of their tendency to appeal to wide audiences and their propensity to be "in" at a particular moment in time. For example, musical fashions that have been "in" at one point or another throughout the past two and half decades in North America include synth-pop, hair-metal or "butt-rock," grunge, rap, hip-hop, R & B, and teen pop. The fortunes of these genres wax and wane with great degrees of irregularity over the years as stars are made overnight only to fall out of grace and slide into popular oblivion in no time. Yet, during the few years when a genre is hot, its power to set the standards in the world of music and popular culture at large can be truly impressive. Take the example of mainstream hip hop: beside the sale of CDs today hip hop artists are featured in movies, TV shows, award contests, fashion, and exercise classes. Moreover, hip hop tunes are used to sell products as diverse as automobiles, milk, soft drinks, and children's toys.

Similarly, consider the teen pop explosion of the late 1990s and early 2000s. At that time, during a span of about five years a seemingly endless succession of "boy bands" and "teen queens" captured the attention of millions of teens worldwide, setting records in sales and in degrees of exposure in the popular media. Popular teen pop icons met with the U.S. President, advertised fast food, performed during the NFL Superbowl's Half Time Show, planned space travel, and graced the cover of every magazine this side of *The Canadian Fly Fisher Magazine*. This concerted effort is noteworthy, as it shows that the majors have a tremendous power to integrate the promotion and sales of fashionable personas across media and across different types of music-related commodities, a power that is magnified by the recent constant increase in adolescents' discretionary income. But the majors also have a tendency to find themselves stuck chasing one another until the system they have created spins out of control and the market reaches exhaustion. When that happens, the clock ticks out on somebody's fifteen minutes of fame. Let us examine how this process works in detail as doing so will shed light on some typical socio-cultural consequences of oligopolic competition.

Love and Commodification: The Case of Teen Pop

In late 2000, I (Phillip) decided to dedicate four months of my life to becoming absorbed in the world of teen pop hits. The research collection process included gathering lyrics of the most popular albums, watching concerts and videos, reading interviews, and gathering as much information about teen pop as I could. After feeling that I gained enough information about teen pop I decided to study in depth the lyrics of fourteen of the most successful albums marketed to teens and pre-teens through the Disney Channel network in the USA. The decision to study song lyrics was motivated by a long-standing tradition in popular music studies which argues that one of the most prominent meanings of music is to be found in lyrics—a tradition influenced in great part by the critical theory of Adorno (Adorno and Hullot-Kentor 2006), who believed that a song's "hook" was its most powerful rhetorical device. Fourteen albums were included in the sample. The Disney Channel at the time offered in its programming music specials, concerts, videos-on-rotation, top-of-the-chart type shows, and interviews featuring at one time or another all of the following fourteen acts: Britney Spears, N'Sync, Backstreet Boys, Christina Aguilera, S Club 7, 98 Degrees, LFO, Jessica Simpson, BBMak, Abba Teens, Aaron

Carter, M2M, Hoku, and Youngstown. Each of these artists' latest full-length record at the time was included in the sample, for a total of 169 songs. Content analysis of the lyrics entailed establishing categories into which segments of songs would be classified, and examining themes of interest within each category.

Following the initial content analysis, a curious finding emerged: the greatest majority of the songs (155 out of 169) talked about love and all of the love songs portrayed love as a type of substance addiction. Research within social psychology and psychology shows that while the substances to which one may become addicted are endless, the features of addiction are remarkable similar as they include craving, feeling "high" under the influence of the substance, obsessing over the lack of the substance itself, becoming dependent, and feeling that the addictive substance is never enough and that more and more is needed to get high again (see Ulman and Paul 2006).

For example, love was portrayed in these songs as something to be craved. Longing for love or desiring a beloved person was both an overwhelming and painful experience generated by the presence of the person or the emotion or its mere fantasy, as in:

> All I want is you (you make me go crazy), all I want is you (you better cross the line), I'm gonna love you right (all I want is you), I want you, I need you.
>
> (Christina Aguilera)

> I wanna be the only thing you need, be the oxygen you breathe, and there's nothing more that I would ever ask for than to be with you, just to be with you.
>
> (Hoku)

Within song lyrics these cravings would generate stress, distortions of reality, illusions, and losses of control that would appear as seemingly omnipotent feelings of knowing how to fix the craving. For instance:

> Boy, I've been watchin' you, and you've been watching me, I know you want me baby, I'm gonna make you see, I'll give you whatcha need.
>
> (Jessica Simpson)

Getting high on love, from either its presence or the mere fantasy of it, was painted as a feeling amazing enough to compel someone to surrender to the power of infatuation, to let go of all inhibitions and to release the will to seek gratification, as in the following:

> I was walking down the street one day, then I saw you I didn't know what to say, your eyes were shining, your smile was so kind, when I saw you I wanted you to be mine.
>
> (M2M)

Yet, getting high on love seems so powerful that one's life becomes unbearable without a fix. Obsession over the craved object of love and feelings of withdrawals from it once the substance is lost are so powerful that the prophecy of love must be fulfilled at all costs:

> You want to run, you want to break free, what you want ain't what you need.
>
> (BBMak)

> I'm not ashamed to tell the world that you really messed up my mind, girl, to me you're like a dream come true, I would rather hurt myself than to ever hurt you. I've never known before a girl I wanted more, the way I want you now, I admit you are the best, and with you I am obsessed and I could never do without.
>
> (Aaron Carter)

Obsession yields dependency, and dependency both begets and arises from feelings of self-insufficiency, as in:

> Without you in my life, baby, I wouldn't be living at all.
>
> (N'Sync)

> Life's too short to live without you, you're my life and I live for your love that you give. When I think, I'd be lost without you, makes me wonder what I did before you.
>
> (S Club 7)

Finally, addiction to love seems to manifest itself in these songs through the desire to demand more from love as an ideal, or from a particular object of love. For instance:

> Baby, baby, we can do more than just talk.
>
> (N'Sync)

While these are clear examples of addiction, it is important not to make too much of these lyrics. It would be not only an exaggeration, but also a mistake, to suggest that being an avid fan of this genre of music will lead to developing addictive dispositions to love or even to be at risk for developing co-dependent relationships. Music listeners are known to play an active role in the interpretation of musical texts and significant musical symbols. To boot, they are often unaware of lyrical passages other than a few hooks, and most of them consume this music while distracted by other activities. And at last, lyrics are only one component of musicality. Melodic instrumental sound is just as important, and visual components (e.g. music videos, physical appeal of performers, etc.) are also relevant. Nevertheless, it is interesting to understand the social significance of these lyrics and how they come to be the way they are. For instance, it is perfectly legitimate to ask why these themes (e.g. love, relationships) emerge among many possible others, and why they emerge in this fashion (i.e. with the characteristics of addiction). Many valid competing explanations exist, yet for pedagogical reasons here we focus on answers dealing with the economic nature of the context in which they are produced.

To begin with, it is interesting to note that several of these songs are written by the same composer, Sweden's Max Martin. Martin is the lyrical genius behind the success of none other than Britney Spears, the Backstreet Boys, N'Sync, and in part, Christina Aguilera. Spears, the Backstreet Boys, and N'Sync also share something else: the same label, Zomba. You may have never heard of Zomba, but you will remember that BMG, which owns Zomba, is one of the "Big 5."

So, what is going on here? From a sociological perspective this concentration of resources and the consequent orchestration of a global marketing strategy can be outlined as follows: a Big 5's subsidiary company recruits talent which turns out to be successful in early market tests. New and similar artists are then quickly signed. The genre's popularity becomes solidified so quickly that in the short run the public will accept almost any act whose music is similar enough to the familiar sound. Almost immediately, competing majors identify the growing market demand and rush to provide audiences with competing offers. New artists—all with the same look and feel—are recruited and promoted. A genre mushrooms and before you know it every major has their Britney and their N'Sync "clones," each commanding an ever-shrinking portion of their audiences' wallets.

As this occurs and carries on over time audiences' enthusiasm and patience also wear thin, while thirst for novelty grows. After all, there is only so much of the same serving that even the least discerning public can stomach. At last, conditions for the complete exhaustion of the success of a trend are in place: stars fall out of place, audiences grow, and a new generation of pop icons and audiences begin to grow together with a new genre to solidify their union. While some of the features of this process would arguably be similar if the market was characterized by perfect pluralism—that is, a balanced competition of several actors—the logic of oligopolic competition inevitably results in some tendencies toward the pseudo-individualization of artists extremely similar to one another, as Adorno remarked, and in the temporary standardization of products, until the market abruptly collapses under the public's unwillingness to support its own conservative impetus.

While the success of similar artists can be explained in large part as the outcome of competing corporate actors imitating one another and relying on sound familiarity as a marketing tool, more needs to be said about the specific quality of the products being sold. As we saw earlier, the lyrics of the hits by Britney Spears, Christina Aguilera, S Club 7, and company share remarkable similarities. Those characteristics are inevitably functional within the context in which they are consumed: adolescents' individual lives are lived in between and betwixt conflicting identities, fragile self-esteem, difficulties establishing and maintaining adult-like relationships, and the various experiences of anxiety that these events evoke. Thus, it is no accident that regardless of the musical genre favourite by teens (e.g. heavy metal, emo, grunge, teen pop, dance, etc.), angst or existential insecurity end up filling the lyrics of music targeted to them (as Bart Simpson once observed, "selling angst to teens is like shooting fish in a barrel").

The qualities of the lyrical content of teen pop also reveal something more fundamental about socio-economic relations: there is a tendency in capitalist societies to foster peoples' desires and inclinations to spend money. An emotional disposition toward symbols such as love that has the qualities of addictive relations is arguably typical of a consumer culture in which both needs and wants are potentially easily satisfied through market-mediated consumption (see Baudrillard 1983). In other words, when people learn that they *can* wish for anything in the world, and that they *can* satisfy every need or want, it becomes logical to expect immediate gratification. This is indeed the seductive and dangerous power of *consumerism*: in a system in which everything is virtually available with the minimum effort (if you consider pulling a credit card out of your wallet a case of minimum effort), those objects of desire that are not necessarily available through minimum efforts (such as people's true love) need to either become commodities themselves or else will frustrate people endlessly (see Baudrillard 1983). And love, indeed, does *tend* to become a commodity in such world. Teen pop songs easily testify to this by portraying love as a substance, an object of consumption and immediate gratification. Thus, lacking love becomes an experience similar to lacking material possessions. For instance, when LFO sing "Without you in my life, I guess the whole thing would be empty," loneliness in the context of a love-deprived life begins to feel very similar to the meanings of poverty in a consumption-deprived existence. Similarly, providing love to others has the feel of providing an endless supply of goods and services to meet their addiction, as in:

> I wanna be there everyday for you, to satisfy your every needs, my baby.
>
> (Backstreet Boys)

And when bands like Youngstown sing passages like the following we are led to conclude that the line between romance and consumption has been significantly blurred:

> You can call me when you want me, if you need a friend you got me I'll be your everything, fulfill your every dream. We can do it automatic; I can freak you with my gadget. I'll be your everything. You'll see I'm everything you want and more. I'll be your gadget, the one you call to make magic, most rap stars live lavish. Got you a Benz for a carriage and even a rock, about 8 to 10 carats but you almost forgot. When we both went to Paris, and you took shots, cause of you, look at all the drinks I got. Think back and look at all the minks you rocked and I know you'll be impressed from the things I got 'cause I'm Mr. Gadget.
>
> (Youngstown)

Cultural commentators like Eva Illouz (1997) have insightfully argued that in consumer society romance tends to become commodified and commodities tend to become romanticized. We do this, for example, when we condemn a lover as "cheap" and when we exclaim things like "I love my new car!" The popular music scene and industry, as the pulse of the times, register these tendencies and perhaps—at the risk of sounding a bit conspiratorial—magnify these trends in hope of securing a more stable position on the market and increasing profits through the sale of even more significant symbols, as we detail in the following sections.

CONSPICUOUS CONSUMPTION

Consumption, as we said, is an important component of our economy. If we did not consume anything, goods would rot and gather dust on shelves, services would go undemanded, production would inevitably cease, and our society's economy would collapse. Without consuming, we would basically all die. However, whereas consumption is inevitable, consumerism is not. *Consumerism* is the name for a cultural system based on the logic of consumption, a logic that equates personal happiness with consumption of commodities and social order and progress with stable increases in the consuming power of groups and individuals. Within sociology, the study of consumerism, or consumer culture, dates as far back as the writings of Marx (in Clarke 2003) and Veblen (2006) and as recently as the writings of Bourdieu (1984) and Featherstone (1991) and others (see Paterson 2005). It is from the critical theoretical thoughts of these scholars that we draw in this section.

Writing at the turn of the twentieth century, Veblen noted that people would regularly engage in a type of consumption that was not driven by the merely instrumental goal of need-satisfaction, but rather directed at a symbolic purpose: self-aggrandizement in the eyes of others. When practiced in order to seek a higher social status or to strike envy in others, consumption—he suggested—is always necessarily *conspicuous*, public, outward-directed, and transparent. Veblen's argument was obviously related to an older Marxist argument, known as *commodity fetishism*. For Marx, commodity fetishism—a characteristic of capitalistic societies—was typical of social relations defined by the value placed in objects. The use of the word "fetish" was provocative and even ironic in this context, but it described well how people seem to crave for commodities not because of their use-value (what instrumental purpose they serve) but for their exchange-value (the market-place value) and consequently its symbolic value.

Later on in the history of sociology another influential thinker, French cultural anthropologist and social theorist Pierre Bourdieu, was able to dissect the complex links existing between the economy and culture. Writing about people's *taste* (how we classify things as aesthetically good or bad) Bourdieu (1984) found that taste serves a unique social function by distinguishing certain people and their forms of taste as refined from certain others whose taste is less socially desirable. Public consumption for Bourdieu was interconnected with the formation and exercise of a unique form of social power, which he called *symbolic capital*. Symbolic capital refers to the honour and prestige granted to someone on the basis of their taste. Symbolic capital and economic capital are closely linked—since things in "good taste" are often expensive—but not necessarily always clearly correlated. For example, some university students may be far from being affluent yet they may display a refined taste for certain cultural practices with relatively high symbolic capital (e.g. theatre and performing arts, adventure travel, ethnic cuisine, etc.). Finally, according to Featherstone (1991)—but also Bourdieu himself—consumption is often directed at the body as a symbolic object of self-expression. For example, people adorn themselves with clothes, accessories, and style their face and body in ways that are consonant with the fashions of the times. "Images of the body beautiful, openly sexual and associated with hedonism, leisure, and display"—Featherstone (1991: 170) writes in an often cited passage—emphasize "the importance of appearance and the 'look.' " And "the look" is indeed meant to be conspicuous. In the following case study we draw upon this background to examine the conspicuous consumption of music-related commodities.

Hot Topic and the Retailing of Musical Material Culture

In a not so distant past, as recently as the 1970s, music-related commodities were often hardly available for purchase. Merchandise such as posters, concert shirts, and even recordings was only irregularly available at best, and even then a fan would be hard pressed to find much for sale in retail stores unless one's beloved singer or band was extremely popular with the masses. As youths' spending power increased and as e-commerce replaced the older system based on catalogue-mailing retail, more and more popular culture-related merchandise became available in urban shops and suburban malls. A clear example of this increased availability is the American chain store "Hot Topic." Founded in 1988 by Orv Madden, Hot Topic has expanded its chain to about 600 retail outlets across the United States and has enjoyed constant revenue growth, estimated at about $650 million in 2004. Featuring both traditional retail and Internet shopping Hot Topic sells anything music-related, including software (CDs, vinyl, etc.), hardware (instruments, DJ equipment, music players), clothing (tops, bottoms, dresses, shoes, underwear), jewellery, belts, hats, bags, infant and toddlers' clothing, and of course gifts (e.g. auto accessories, pet fashion, stickers, patches, pins, stationery, print media, room décor, keychain, lighters, candy, toys, and action figures), and accessories (e.g. cosmetics, bath and body fragrances, gloves and arm-warmers, hair colors and hair goods, hosiery, scarves, bandanas, shoelaces, socks, sunglasses, ties, watches, and wristbands).

Hot Topic's catalogue is seemingly depthless; it almost feels as if every major and relatively minor contemporary rock band has at least one or two items in most of the categories above. With some background and subcultural know-how a consumer can literally walk into a store as a "square" and walk out with a new and refreshingly cool body, identity, and style. Let us then do this, as a hypothetical exercise Joe and I will be the "lab rats." Let us assume, for example, that a friend of ours whom we happen to think is pretty hip is into Green Day. We like our friend and we like his style, and because we're ready for a makeover we decide to go shopping. Right away Joe and I go to the nearest Hot Topic outlet and start browsing around.

Generally, I am into classic dark and earth tone colors, whereas Joe prefers more histrionic stuff. I cannot help falling in love with this dark button up shirt I find: 65% polyester and 35% cotton, this black short-sleeved shirt features a grey heart-shaped grenade on the right shoulder and a gray Green Day logo at waist height. Since I really dig the heart-shaped grenade—I don't know why, I guess because it's just so sensitive and yet rebellious—I am going to grab a heart grenade keychain, a heart grenade ID case, an army cadet hat featuring the beloved symbol, as well as a cloth wristband, a lighter for the smokes that I really don't smoke, a heart grenade belt buckle, an army-style necklace, and a green bandana to go with the whole shebang. While Joe looks around for his stuff, I am going to find a pair of pants and shoes to match.

After going through some of the same piles of clothes and accessories Joe realizes that, even though he likes the style, he really cannot wear the same stuff as me—or else we might end up having to phone each other before going out together to make sure that we are not wearing matching outfits; how embarrassing—it would completely destroy our originality. So, after browsing a bit more Joe gets into this really cool heavy metal look that seems to fit his thirst for something unique. He starts out by trying on a black Deftones ball cap with a white stitch around the bill, a zipper on the front, and the band's logo on the back, but even though he likes the idea of looking like a heavy metal fan, he feels like he does not want to wear a ball hat. After some more hesitation, he is suddenly struck with awe as he lays his eyes on the look of his dreams: black vinyl five-pocket pants, Slipknot's T.U.K. black double lace robot-style sole boots, and a fearsome long black grommet coat with a zipper running from neck to below the beltline and metal studs and buckles encircling the chest and back. Plus, to truly scare the devil out of the neighborhood's kids, he snatches the Slipknot 133 latex mask, featuring a grey metal zipper across the mouth, and a four dozen ten-inch plastic spikes exploding out of his skull. To top it all up he adds to his cart a Slipknot skateboard for easy commuting to his favorite 7–11 hangout from his university office.

Awesome! We're good to go represent! As we proceed to charge our new identity onto our credit cards, the friendly clerk—referring to the tune playing in the background on the store's stereo—says to me: "Don't you just love their last CD?" "Totally amazing"—I reply, then pausing just a second to hear some the lyrics going: ". . . Don't wanna be an American idiot. Don't want a nation under the new media. And can you hear the sound of hysteria? The subliminal mind fuck America." "Yeah," I add, "and what they say is totally true!" "I know, it's right on"—she replies—"Well, have a good one guys!" "Yeah, take it easy"—I mumble as I walk out. "Dude"—Joe looks at me and mutters from behind the mask he decided to wear out—"Who was that playing in the store?" "Beats me, bro"—I answer—"I said that just to be nice, but I really didn't like it that much, it sounded like poseur rock, you know what I mean? But hey, what about Slipknot, didn't you get any of their CDs?" "Nah . . ."—Joe concludes—"I'm more into the music of Green Day, anyway."

What this scenario goes to show is that in this case Joe and I (and others like us) fetishize music-related commodities. We do not care much about the actual sound of the music, and for the most part we are even unaware of musical conventions associated with the scenes to which we claim membership. Music in this case for us is not something to appreciate in deep listening or a form of self-expression that we can produce by playing our own instruments. Rather, music for us is a system of objects, a *structure of commodities* with symbolic values attached to them. For us, the music of Slipknot and Green Day has no use value—in other words, it does not matter to us as musical sound in itself—but it does have symbolic value since by purchasing the "look" associated with it and by conspicuously consuming such commodities we can establish our identity as fans (albeit, fans who try a tad too hard admittedly).

Music-related commodities have an almost automatic affiliation with *subcultures of consumption*. It is no accident that commodities belonging to the same consumer axis of signification (say, for example, the category of punk-related clothes and accessories) have a great degree of internal coherence. It makes perfect sense, for example, for a Slipknot fan to wear a scary trench coat and a mask, or for a Green Day fan to sport a casual but hip button up shirt and loose fit black denims. The *homology* among these symbols allows members of the same tribe to establish a sense of uniqueness from the rest of the world while maintaining a stable and value-congruent *collective identity*. As Bourdieu would suggest, this is possible because taste is a relatively coherent disposition that is easily transferred from one object to another. If taste were not so coherent, there would be nothing strange in a Slipknot fan wearing Jennifer Lopez perfume and a "Stuff by Duff" waist belt, yet it is clear that there is, and any fan who claims authentic membership to a subcultural group knows to stay well away from purchasing consumer items that would lessen the symbolic capital that he/she enjoys within the community.

Of course, our claim to authenticity is questionable and perhaps the object of a longer discussion that we can tackle here (see, however, Chapter 7 on globalization). After all, subcultures have always made distinctions among poseurs, weekenders, and authentic members (see Muggleton 2002). Yet, in the end it seems more and more difficult these days to establish who is authentic and by what criteria. In fact, can one be an authentic member of a commodified subculture? If we go back to Benjamin and his ideas on the loss of the aura of original artistic expression by way of mechanical reproduction, we can easily conclude that within a system based on the logic of consumption and the prevalence of the copy, authenticity seems almost utopian and dependent on symbols, rather than what symbols stand for.

In sum, what we have learnt here is that within a market economy and consumerist culture self-expression is almost always inevitably mediated through the conspicuous consumption of commodities. Within such a system, symbolic value often tends to matter as much or even more than the use value of music. As individual lives become more and more focused around self-expression, the consumer system gains increasing power due to its ability to provide individuals with an increasingly larger volume of identity-expressing symbols rich with potential for enriching one's symbolic capital.

MUSIC AS A COMMERCIAL TECHNOLOGY

As sociologist of music Tia DeNora (2000) has found, people use music with a great variety of goals in a large number of different contexts. For example, music is used to "pump up" one's attitude during aerobic work-outs, to create a romantic atmosphere ideal for love-making, to communicate one's gender identity to significant others, and so forth. When music is used this way, it works as a tool, a technique, a strategy for the satisfaction of goals other than enjoyment from music listening itself. When we understand music as a means to an end, we can conceptualize it as a technology. Of course, the technological function of music does not prevent aesthetic appreciation of music itself (for example, you may get *both* a better work-out and a deeper respect for the band out of a Metallica-soundtracked weight-lifting session), but the point here is that music can become functional, rather than good or bad in and of itself. Because music has this malleability, it can be sold as commodity with little or no apparent regard to the aesthetic ideal of originality or genuine artistic self-expression.

Music is not the only technology used to communicate information or to change the definition of a situation in everyday life. As Arlie Hochschild (1983) found in her classic study of flight attendants, public displays of emotions are also used as technologies to maximize customer satisfaction and therefore economic goals. Hochschild called this *emotional labor*. Certain forms of music are also used as emotional techniques. Think, for example, of the music (generally soft rock or new age) piped into dentists' offices or massage parlours, or the soothing new age played upon airplane landing and takeoff on long flights.

The point here, in sum, is that *music as a public form of emotional expression* may play, and often does play, a role in defining a social situation as economically profitable for the social agents that choose to adopt it in such instrumental fashion. When this occurs, we may say that music becomes a commercial, and in certain cases corporate, technology.

As more and more companies realize the potential of using music as commercial technology, music comes to play an increasingly greater role in what Hochschild would call the *commercialization of human feelings*—that is, the buying and selling of emotions in the way that we have examined earlier in relation to teen pop lyrics. Also, music begins to play a more important role in the solidification of social structures and public order. This use of music as instrumental means is not new. Think for example of how nations have used hymns to cement collective allegiance to patriotic ideals and collective causes. Yet, what is truly unique about the use of music in this fashion in post-industrial society is its pliability in rendering almost any social context one in which consumption of commercial goods and services can and should take place. It is to this functionality of music across different everyday life situations that we now turn our attention.

Music and the Sound of the Cash Register

When most people are asked to name music produced and used for purely commercial purposes they can promptly name muzaak—ambient music originally made by the homonymous corporation frequently found in such environments as airports, airplanes, elevators, shopping malls, grocery stores, and such. Hardly anyone, however, buys muzaak for their own private consumption except in those cases when ambient music is actually aesthetically complex enough to gather a cult following, such as Brian Eno's album "Music for Airports" album, for example. Yet, we tend to forget that there is a vast variety of musical forms produced and consumed to achieve an aim other than, or in addition to, musical satisfaction itself.

Take, for example, Christmas music. While there is no doubt that there are some people out there who *really do enjoy* Christmas music and who even collect Christmas compilations and albums, the truly interesting (at least in the context of this chapter) social function of Christmas music is to put people in a "holiday mood." Imagine yourself driving in suburban weekend traffic on a snowy or stormy day to score as many special deals as possible on your holiday gift-shopping list. As your emotions are overwhelmed by thoughts of piling-up credit card bills, things you'd rather do on a Saturday afternoon instead of looking for an elusive parking spot, and the ever growing number of people in your extended family and circle of friends to buy for . . . bam! Here comes Frank Sinatra's unmistakable voice singing on the radio "Have yourself a merry little Christmas," and for at least three minutes and thirty seconds you actually do get the feel that this is indeed a special time of the year.

Holiday music is a big business. At the time of writing, Amazon.com, for example, gives its online customers 9,797 options for the holiday music shopper. Some of the more popular Christmas recordings include albums by jazzy Canadian Diana Krall, and *American Idol* runner-up Clay Aiken. Despite the more or less serious claim to musical legitimacy by these two candidates, the odd-ballness of a great number of Christmas albums exposes the dubiousness of the commercial Christmas concept. Indeed, it seems that just about every mainstream group or solo performer these days has a holiday album out on the market, including (in a revealing parodying demonstration of the case we are making) *South Park*'s own "Mr. Hankey"—an animated and often high-on-drugs poo turd donning a Christmas hat and brightly colored scarf singing renditions and remixes of such classics (?) as "Merry fucking christmas," "Dead, dead, dead," and "Christmas time in hell."

Aside from the obvious aberrations such as the one above, many commercial Christmas albums truly do reveal the expansionary logic of capitalism. The insistence of Christmas albums on carols, folk songs, and other jingles and tunes that have been in the public domain for decades and decades goes to show how consumerist culture is slowly replacing traditionally gratis musical performances, like singing on the street (now most carollers are hired by public or private groups) or family chorus-singing. Radio has adapted to this logic too, as several of the soft-rock oriented stations now feature all-day long Christmas music around that magical time of the year. While not music-related, the phenomenon of the media market replacing "authentic" objects with commodities is also exemplified by those television channels which during the holiday season broadcast 24/7 burning, crackling logs (supposedly intended to be played in the living room background, as a substitute for the fireplace, rather than as a form of reality TV on pyromania). The point here, in sum, is that a "mood" is now for sale.

Christmas itself, as the story goes, is a holiday constructed by a loose coalition of interests and the agents that represent them. Most historians agree that the birth of Jesus Christ happened with great probability around mid-March. Yet those who do celebrate Christmas celebrate it on the 25th of December as that date was chosen with the focused intent to compete with the popularity of the pagan festival of the Winter Solstice. The celebration of Christmas as both a religious and a commercial holiday began to take root in North America only around the late nineteenth century, and it was only through the carefully concerted efforts of city officials and commercial groups that Christmas as a family and shopping extravaganza—mixed with slowly receding religious significance—took hold over the public debauchery that earlier celebration rituals called for (see Nissenbaum 1997).

If Christmas music indeed can be shown to work in creating a Christmas "mood" that contributes at least in part to the maintenance of public order and the growth of the world's economy (after all, economists agree that consumer indexes for the month of December serve as efficient measures of the economic wealth of a consumer economy), what must be said is that Christmas music is by far not the only type of commercial holiday music. Halloween, Hanukkah, and Kwanzaa music albums are also good commercial enterprises. For example, the Amazon.com catalog shows that about 400 musical products are available in the three categories combined. Halloween—itself another commercial smorgasbord for the candy industry—music, with its spooky, ghostly, and ghoulish sounds and lyrics seems to work just as well as a technology of fear, albeit perhaps with less cultural significance for society.

Beside holiday times, music works as a commercial technology in other cases. Again, Amazon.com (which despite appearances, we guarantee is NOT sponsoring this chapter) features in its catalog such functional music as wedding, self-help, nostalgia, exercise, and sports music. For example, the wedding music category includes compilations of "ethnic" favorites such as "The Italian Wedding" and "The Celtic Wedding," as well as songs exclusively written to be played during certain moments of the wedding ritual (like "A song for my daughter on her wedding day" meant to be played for the mother and groom dance during the wedding reception). The self-help category (and please, read this list slowly and try and imagine what these actually sound like!) includes music for healing, meditation, inner peace, sleep, relaxation, self-hypnosis, accelerated learning, weight loss, self-esteem enhancement, achieving success, attracting prosperity, breaking addiction, and, incredibly enough, even more.

Nostalgia music, as the name itself suggests, is a commercial technology meant to evoke nostalgic feelings. Objects of musical nostalgia include historical eras (like decades), events (like wars), or historical figures in popular culture. Exercise music includes music for physical activities such as military cadence running, abdominal crunching, yoga, aerobics, power-walking, tae bo, step, stretching, and country work-out (which includes songs to sweat to such as "Running Bear," "Shut up and drive," and "Honky tonk dancing machine"). Finally, the sports category includes soundtracks written for sports as a whole (like wrestling), and sports teams, and is meant to incite, cheer, and strike feelings of collective pride. These examples show that when music is produced, distributed, and consumed to satisfy goals other than appreciation of its aesthetic qualities, its instrumental functions work as commercial technologies marketed and sold to change definitions of social situations and in order to reproduce, imitate, or alter individual feelings and collective emotional dispositions. Music as commercial technology is increasingly typical of a post-industrial society in which individuals exist as consumers and in which rituals are almost exclusively mediated by market relations.

CONCLUSION

What we have demonstrated in this chapter is that music plays an important role in our economy. Music is an important aspect of life-style, and because within our consumer culture lifestyles are based on consumption—conspicuous or not—music inevitably feeds into eco-nomic cycles. Within a market economy and a consumerist society music is also commodified, and consequently many of the feelings it evokes or represents are also commodified. This is not to say that music can never be mixed with economic concerns. Artists are human beings and they too need to consume and feed their families. Yet, as we hope we showed, there is an important difference between producing music in order to sell it, and producing music in order to sell it off.

4

THE COMMUNITY AND THE POLITY

If a man were permitted to make all the ballads, he need not care who should make the laws of a nation.

[Andrew Fletcher, 1997 [1703])

As Balliger (1999) rightly notes, within the field of popular music studies the notion of "politics" immediately denotes political songs or protest music. In the world of pop music too, it seems that when politics and music are explicitly mixed, a listener is in for either tunes that work as a "struggle against dominant institutions like the state and economic system" (Balliger 1999:57) or for music that serves to support existing values—like official national anthems or patriotic hymns such as "God Bless America" or Gilles Vigneault's "Gens du Pais," Quebec's anthem. To limit a discussion of politics in music to these genres is, however, unwise. More insightfully instead, we can say that music (popular and otherwise) has a political *structure* and *polity-forming capacity* of its own.

In the case of the contemporary popular music industry, this structure is generally understood as a *political oligarchy*. As defined earlier, an oligarchy is an arrangement of power in which only few social agents have the faculty to rule a mass of many. Pop music's oligarchy manifests itself through powerful commercial alliances among music production labels. These labels control the global market by promoting unlimited consumer access to musical genres and artists, but by restricting such access in actual practice. Such restriction is achieved via control of both production and distribution through the standardization of popular music sounds. Because of pop music's close relation with the rest of pop culture (movies, fashion, lifestyle, etc.), this oligarchy has the capacity to draw and even shape like-minded audiences characterized by similarities in outlooks, values, and taste. Popular music, in its capacity to draw and form communities may then be said to be a social and political force.

Politics enters music, and music enters politics, in numerous and often subtle ways. A sociological approach to music might find political values even in songs that have nothing to do with patriotism or protest. For example, even a harmlessly apolitical hook like "NaNaNaNaNa" sung by the bubbliest of bubbly pop stars has a deep cultural and political significance. According to someone like Theodor Adorno (Adorno and Hullot-Kentor 2006), the infantilization of pop songs is both a symptom and the cause of the formation of a *mass* culture. A mass culture is one in which people's sense of taste has been standardized by a culture industry keen on preserving the political and economic status quo rather than in the elevation of artistic and political consciousness. If Adorno and colleagues are right, then politics is everywhere in popular music—despite the fact that we are sometimes oblivious to the hidden political realities of musical production, distribution, or consumption. It should be interesting to uncover some of the more profound political meanings within the world of popular music. Following our customary approach of examining the mundane in order to appreciate the deep connection between music and society, in this chapter we examine the relationship between popular music and politics, polity, and community by taking into consideration the multiple meanings of "politics" in popular music studies. We begin by examining the practice of cardboard CD packaging as a way of posing alternatives to the political, economic, and aesthetic oligarchy of the music industry. We then analyze some subtle parallels between *American Idol* and Presidential elections in the U.S. We conclude with a reflection on the socializing properties of music by positing the dispersed audiences of the children's musical cartoon *Dora the Explorer* as a community with shared values and habits of thought. Our pedagogical goal in this chapter is to explain three important concepts often used in sociological parlance: ideology, institutions, and community.

IDEOLOGY

There exist several different sociological understandings of the concept of ideology, yet the most basic definition simply views ideology as a set of ideas about something. By ideas, here we mean things such as values, beliefs, and ideals about social conduct. Within sociology and related disciplines the concept of ideology is inevitably a social one, in the sense that ideologies are always systems of ideas about how society is and about how it should be. Moreover, ideologies are social in the sense that they are shared by groups of people. Of course, by suggesting that ideologies are shared, we are not implying that they are shared by everyone; as a matter of fact, ideologies and the groups who support them are often in conflict with one another. Yet, the point that more than one individual, somewhere, at some point in time, will share an ideology is a powerful one in and of itself, and an even more powerful one in light of its consequences.

When people share an ideology, they tend to forget that alternative ideologies exist and that these alternatives are as plausible as their preferred view. What makes ideologies so powerful is that they have a tendency to legitimize behavior and to become reified. Take, for example, the idea (and related beliefs, values, assumptions, behaviours, etc.) that classical music is "better"—that is, more refined, sophisticated, enlightened, etc.—than pop music. Ultimately there is no way of proving this to be an unchallengeable truth, yet the idea is strong enough to become so "real" in its consequences, so much a matter of fact, so "reified" that for the most part public schools all over the world abstain from teaching popular music courses (and often even formally condemn it as a negative influence) and focus instead on instructing children to play "classical" instruments as part of their art curriculum. In this example we can see how an ideology—the idea that classical music is inherently more valuable than popular music—*legitimizes* certain educational practices and delegitimizes others. The more an ideology becomes legitimized, the more it tends to be experienced as an incontrovertible truth and not as mere opinions, outlooks, or ideas. Indeed, the "fact" that classical music "does good things" to children, and the "fact" that rap or speed metal "do bad things" to them becomes a belief *reified*—that is, materialized—deep enough that parents "caught" exposing their wee ones to 50 Cent or Anthrax promptly need to account for their "irresponsible" behavior.

In general sociological terms, people in power have at least two means of maintaining their privileges: forceful means and symbolic means. Music is hardly ever used in forceful ways—though it has been used as such in the past (for example, Ontario police once blared out "boy band" music to disperse a crowd of street protesters and Guantanamo Bay military police have been known to play loud death metal to scare inmates). For the most part, music is instead used as a symbolic force, in other words, as a medium for ideology.

According to many critical theorists, the ideology that is most often present in popular music is that of conservativism. Conservativism is the ideology supported by the alliance of commercial groups who hold the political and economic power within a capitalist society. For obvious reasons these groups have a keen interest in maintaining the status quo. The best way to maintain such a state of affairs is to sell people something they want to buy and at the same time something they want to believe in. Italian sociologist Antonio Gramsci referred to this societal state and process as *hegemony*. Critical theorists explain that pop music appreciation tends to work in hegemonic fashion by resulting in the appeasement of people into accepting and even supporting the status quo—whether they do this consciously or without being aware. For example, due to its merry repetitiveness, catchy simplicity, and inoffensive superficiality, the consumption of pop music is believed to lead to the regression of the listener to child-like mental states—a regression which serves the purpose of distracting individuals away from realizing the depth of the social conditions that oppress them and others. This hegemonic function of music—that is, its complicit role in supporting the status quo—has been traditionally condemned both in light of its political consequences and in light of the actual means used, that is the texts, sounds, and performances that made such music so "bad."[1]

In contrast, popular music that is "good" in itself and good in terms of its consequences for people is autonomous music; or at least, so this critical theoretical argument goes. According to this counter-hegemonic ideology, which we could call an ideology of *resistance*, autonomous, independent, genuine music is believed to be synonymous with authenticity—something which is highly valued (at least in the surface) by many people of character and especially, and perhaps stereotypically, by artists. Autonomy and authenticity mean many different things, but they generally entail independence from shallow values—such as fame, economic success, political collusion, etc.—that "corrupt" the ideal purity of musical expression. Autonomous and authentic music is often political protest music: songs that work as "cultural alternatives to the lifestyles of the "mainstream." This type of music often falls into one of the following categories: protest against oppression or exploitation; aspiration toward a better and more just life; satire of those in power; philosophical reflection; commemoration of popular struggles; inspiration for collective movements; tribute to martyrs; expression of working-class solidarity; and critical social

---

1 With regard to "bad" music, see the excellent collection of reflections on "the music we love to hate" in Washburne and Derno (1999).

commentary. Regardless of the actual category that a musical perform-ance, recording, or genre may fall into, autonomous and authentic music intends to solicit or arouse support for a movement or cause, create solidarity and cohesion, promote awareness or evoke solutions to social problems, and simply to provide hope.

Autonomy and authenticity sound like good values, but in actuality they are hardly achievable. A sociological understanding of autonomy leads us to find that music-making is for the most part dependent on strategic compromises and negotiation. As Becker (1982) has demon-strated, the production of art is a complex joint act between vast num-bers of people with different yet related goals. Despite the myth of the lonely genius doing music on his/her own, like all social activities music-making is a collective accomplishment. As we can see below in the case of Montreal-based production label Constellation Records, despite a strong ideology of autonomy and authenticity, certain negoti-ations and compromises with the system are inevitable.

Politics, Technology, and Indie Music

Any new technological medium of musical expression "changes the way in which we experience music" (Shuker 2001: 51) and poses "both constraints and opportunities in terms of the organisation of produc-tion" (ibid.). As Shuker has convincingly stated, the history of music in the Western hemisphere is marked by a series of shifts from oral and live performance to musical notation and then onward to recording and dissemination through a multitude of media. From a related per-spective, music's history can be said to be one of the technological transitions from a context in which the human voice was the only technology of production to one in which the voice is accompanied by a variety of sonorous technologies. If we agree that singing is a technique of expression and that musical sound is a technic or medium of expression, we should agree that music itself is a form of technology.

Just like music, politics too is a form of technology. To understand this claim we ought to begin by understanding technology broadly as a general body of knowledge comprised of "how-to" specifications for action. Of course a technology is not just a collection of tools and "how-to" specifications on how to operate those tools, but also a body of values specifying how tools should be used and for what purposes. Understood this way, the difference between politics and technology is tenuous: both politics and music are technologies of expression. Polit-ics focuses on the expression of political value and the implementation of social ideas through political means, and music focuses on the expression of aesthetic value and orients itself to sound as the tool through which expressiveness can be achieved. Politics and technology (and therefore music) are indeed inextricable. In this section we examine how technology and specific musical techniques acquire political importance and more precisely how different forms of technology contribute to the formation and maintenance of political boundaries between communities.

We begin in Montreal, Canada, where a relatively obscure music production company known as Constellation Records has made an interesting choice for the material with which all the CDs in their catalog are packaged: cardboard. Cardboard is a material that, once treated and adapted for the purpose of CD-packaging can constitute an alternative to the plastic generally used for the manufacturing of CD jewel cases. But why do so, when plastic is obviously more time-efficient for labor, more durable, and cheaper? And how is this choice for cardboard sociologically significant? According to the masterminds of this strategy at Constellation:

> Mechanical reproduction, whether digital or analogue with regard to the music itself, whether at the local die-cutter or silk-screener with regard to packaging and printing, is accessible technology and allows for the duplication and dissemination of cultural work at the micro-level, even if the macroscopic potentials of the technology machine, with respect to art no less than labour practice or weaponry, are terrifying. It's all about maintaining a human scale. Fin-de-siècle capitalism both facilitates and threatens independent production, and the key for us is to utilise those technologies that capitalism itself has marginalised and dispersed in order to create cultural objects that are inherently critical of the system. To the extent this condemns us to pursuing quality at the expense of quantity, it is a fate to which we willingly submit.
>
> (http://www.cstrecords.com/html/manifesto.html)

Constellation's technological position is a stance for difference from the mainstream, independence, and authenticity. These are common values in "indie" music—a synonym for independent, that is, independent from economic, political, aesthetic, and technological pressures from the rest of the music industry and mainstream music and society. Indie music labels like Constellation attempt to build unique communities built on the political (or apolitical?) philosophy of punk and post-punk in order to separate themselves from other musical communities and exercise resistance against pressures to conform.

It is not always easy to do so. While it is true that by choosing techniques and material like cardboard over conventional plastic Constellation artisans and artists tend to achieve a certain sense of difference—a distinct identity, if you will—it is also true that dealing with recycled cardboard packaging means involving complex networks of local artisans, craftsmen, and environmentally-sensitive local business suppliers as well as applying more intensive human labor (such as cutting, folding, trimming, and drawing), which results in increasing costs and possibly lowering consumer demand. Yet, this also results in rejecting plastic with the corrupting tendencies it embodies, and allowing "the sensibility of the music [to be] reflected in and reinforced by the tactility of the package that contains it" (http://www.cstrecords.com/html/pckg.html). This is very much ideology in practice.

Constellation's alternative approach to technology does not end with cardboard. Constellation's work is as political as its packaging technology. Take, for example, its politics of distribution. Far from representing a mere technical process of getting live or recorded sound from a point of origin to a destination, the process of distribution needs to take into consideration the geographic distribution of retail stores and the clients that frequent these. After all, could you reject plastic and then feel coherent about shipping off your cardboard-packaged records to a suburban shopping mall? Rather than malls Constellation, similarly to other indie labels, then mostly attempts to rely on a network of Mom-and-Pop stores across Canada and the United States, as well as low-budget site Internet distribution and marketing via word-of-mouth and underground zine coverage. Obviously this keeps Constellation's profits to a minimum, but it also allows its artists to remain relatively free from the pressure of making marketable music.

Take, for example, its most famous band, "Godspeed! You Black Emperor" (GYBE). GYBE remains keen on touring small venues, playing on pitch-dark stages to avoid emphasizing their image more than their sound, refusing interviews with most media outlets, and obstinately refusing to compromise their aesthetic and political ideologies of resistance, no matter how obscure and controversial these can get. GYBE, a nine-piece, multi-instrumental symphony-rock orchestra has to date recorded four albums, "f#a#?," "slow riot for new zero Canada," "lift yr. skinny fists like antennas to heaven," and the latest "Yanqui U.X.O." which have intrigued a growing (but not too fast) number of fans across the world. Their favorite technology of sound is something describable as apocalyptic gloom, doomed nostalgia, and melodic urban utopia in which their voiceless rhythms re-cover tape loops of street recordings, bigots' rants, corporate mini-mart in-store public announcements, and ethnic chants. Rather than "hooks," "choruses," or screamed verses, their few, sparse, unsystematic instances of prose involve found-by-accident passages of unscripted life or distant narrators' voices mumbling decentered poetry such as:

> The car is on fire and there is no driver at the wheel and the sewers are all muddied with a thousand lonely suicides. And a dark wind blows. The government is corrupt and we are all soul-mate drunks with our radio on and the curtains drawn. We're trapped in the belly of this horrible machine and the machine is bleeding to death.[2]

Through their music, instrumental sounds, and lyrics, GYBE and other Constellation bands are outspokenly critical of commodified and standardized musical and political expression typical of post-industrial neo-liberal society. As Constellation declares in its manifesto, through these choices

> [It has] attempted to evolve one possible model for the recovery of an independent music ethic, hoping to summon some real sense of indie rock in spite of its reduction to a branded slogan through corporate co-optation, its laissez-faire attitude towards the market and the means of production, and all the facile irony that helps pave the path for these content-negating trends.
> (http://www.cstrecords.com/html/cowards.html)

For example, by privileging the production of an immediate and almost "live" (as "live" as recordings can get) sound Constellation condemns commodified duplication and mechanical reproduction. Furthermore, Constellation's music is openly political and at times their rhetoric is purely inflammatory. For example, parody plays a great role in the music of GYBE. Whether their sounds are overlapped by recorded in-store messages of corporate chain highway mini-marts, raging rants of street reactionary, or paranoid poetry embracing the value of armed self-defense, GYBE continually use parody to laugh at others and occasionally even at the solemn seriousness of their own scene.

In other instances Constellation's random noise adds to the cacophony of their politics, yet sounding like beautiful harmonies to those who slow down to listen. Take, for example, GYBE's recording "*Yanqui U.X.O.*" (Yankee Unexploded Ordinance). Following the irrational and yet motivated aesthetics of punk protest "Yanqui U.X.O." is a wordless

---

2 Godspeed! You Black Emperor. "The Dead Flag Blues (Intro)," *f♯a♯∞*.

condemnation of American military interventionism. The music alone, in its sheer symphonic violence of ups and downs resembling the rhythms of airplanes rising and bombs falling, does all the talking. Yet, at the periphery of the sound, on the very cardboard in which the disc is enveloped, GYBE's belligerent overtones are most audible. A folder depicting a hammer inexorably squelching the word hope written in relief in the midst of white flying chimeras reinforces the impression of muted silence imposed by the American bomber featured on the cover. The disc itself bears the inscription: "rockets fall on Rocket Falls" and "motherfucker = redeemer"—an obvious indictment of turn-of-the-century U.S. foreign policy. "U.X.O."—GYBE adds—"is unexploded ordinance is landmines is cluster bombs. All of it mixed by god's pee." The back side of the cover art blurs music and politics even more. There a chart links Sony, AOL Time-Warner, Universal, and BMG to shared financial holdings in the military/weaponry industry: a controversial but certainly thought-provoking addition to the idea of the politico-industrial-military complex. GYBE's and Constellation's ideology is one that is deeply counter-hegemonic and built on values of autonomy and authenticity as resistance—a common yet vanishing strategy in the world of trademarked alternative rock (see Moore 2005).

Is this the epitome of coherent authenticity and autonomy? Well, maybe for the most part. But walk down to your local suburban mall, step into the music store, and look for GYBE or other Constellation bands. Yes, you'll find them. Maybe even a couple of bucks cheaper that you would down at the hipster music store downtown. Is this the irony of assimilation? The price of resistance? The testament to the impossibility of authenticity? The corruptive necessity of practicing a politics of autonomy? Or all of the above? The irony of it all is that for audiences the authenticity of Constellation remains, at best, an impression. There is ultimately no way of telling whether Constellation is strategically trying to convey a contrived impression of authenticity (and thus further commodifying alternative rock (see Frank and Weiland 1997; Moore 2005)) or its intentions are genuine. In the end, as we discuss in our chapter on race, gender, and class in relation to the class performance of Avril Lavigne, it all depends on how good a performance is, and whether an audience buys it.

INSTITUTION

The most obvious reference of the word institution is a mental asylum. Yet within sociology the word "institution" has several abstract meanings, some of which are not easily understood by students. Let us begin to explain the sociological significance of institution as if indeed we were referring to mental institutions and explore that concept from the angle of popular music. To do so, let us assume that you decide to start a new band featuring the absence of any obvious trace of melody. As if the oddness of your sound was not enough, you decide to add to your tracks extremely loud distorted recordings of half a dozen trains asynchronously operating their rusty brakes in the midst of a windstorm. Next, you decide that you and your band members ought to wear chicken uniforms both on and off stage. Finally, you write lyrics featuring nothing but Simglish words (the type of English featured on the video game "The Sims") and as the band leader you proceed to scream those through a megaphone while a back-up singer rhythmically barks the world "sailor" in a phoney Australian accent.

Now imagine that by sheer accident your manager books you for a Christmas show at an old folks' home. While you can probably manage to leave the stage and the scene without actually being institutionalized, chances are that most of the members will want to have you committed. But why would they? The answers to this question are simple but they hold the key to a better understanding of the concept of institution.

First, your audience deemed you offensive because your band does not resemble—in the terms of the style of your performance—the musical styles to which they are accustomed. *Custom* is an important component of the concept of institution. People believe that customs are important because they represent long-standing ways of doing things, and institutions indeed have a clear historical impetus. After all, to break away from a custom means to tear an institution apart. Second, your reception among your audience is poor because in their belief you lack a *social organization* that supports and respects what you do. The musical industry as a whole is an example of such a social organization. Its support of custom is manifested through sale charts, awards, multi-year contracts, etc. So, because in your audience's mind your band is not backed by such organizational support, you come across to them as lacking institutional approval and therefore you are worthy of condemnation. What we have learned here is that these two components, *institution as custom* and *institution as recognized social organization*, are the two most important aspects of the sociological definition of institution.

As you can easily imagine, the formation and upholding of customs and social organization are political matters. Institutions, in other words, have political force: a type of power with an inevitable conservative bias which can be as simple as the respect owed to custom. Custom is a paramount concern for all artists. In fact, no matter how innovative

and even revolutionary a form of art may be, it has to deal with institutional gatekeepers (Frith 1991) who enforce existing ways of doing
things and existing criteria of what is good and bad. Art institutions are
known by sociologists as "art worlds" (Becker 1982: x): "network[s] of
people whose cooperative activity, organized via their joint knowledge
of conventional means of doing things, produce[s] the kind of art
works that art world is known for." While institutionalization makes
life difficult for original expression—and unfortunately that is too bad
for you and your chicken uniform-donning band members—it allows
for familiar and customary performances to register more easily with
audiences. From all of this it follows that, despite its aura of originality,
much art needs to be conventional to be successful. As we discuss
below, the case of *American Idol* shows this phenomenon quite clearly;
not only is the music featured on *American Idol* customary, but its very
codes as a cultural performance draw from deep-rooted institutions of
American society and from a vision of audiences/constituents as customers. To boot, the show itself in its sheer duration and repeated
exposure to emerging artists is an exercise in creating "idols" as
institutions.

American Idol: Rock the Vote (but not too loud)!

If you have never heard of the televised singing contest known as *American Idol* in the U.S., or *Canadian Idol* in Canada, *Australia Idol* in
Australia, *Pop Idol* in the U.K., or any of the national "Idol" competi-
tions featured in more than fifteen countries around the world, you
must live under a rock. The popularity of *American Idol* is the stuff that
TV producers' dreams are made of. Over the past few years, broadcast-
ings of the show on the Fox Network in the U.S. have completely
outlasted, outwitted, and outposted all other reality shows as well as
other mega-TV-events such as the Olympics, the NBA and NHL play-
offs, the Grammy Awards, and the Academy Awards. *American Idol* is,
without exaggeration, the biggest musical phenomenon of the twenty-
first century.

Despite the fact that featured songs change from country to country,
the show is remarkably consistent in its format across the world. Generally the contest begins with early auditions hosted in a country's
major urban centers. Hopeful contestants sing off against tens of thousands of competitors by performing before a panel of judges anonym-
ous to TV audiences (this very first phase is never broadcast) a cappella
a song of their choice. After passing this preliminary round—either
thanks to their good singing skills, comedic potential, or thanks to the
human interest of their personal biographies—a handful of contestants
are invited to sing for a panel of celebrity judges. In the United States

the panel is composed of singer Paula Abdul and producers Randy Jackson and Simon Cowell. Together, and in often in dramatic spite of one another's preferences, the celebrity judges select and invite a small sample of lucky contenders to compete in a series of singing tasks in "Hollywood," California (most often this round is held in Pasadena). During these and later auditions the judges make further cuts until a smaller group of twelve is selected for the final rounds of the show. Week after week the lucky dozen punctually lose one not-so-lucky contestant who is voted "off" by viewers casting their ballot through a wide array of interactive media, until at last one winner is crowned the country's singing "Idol" in the season's finale. In what follows we examine how *American Idol* epitomizes political values central to America's political culture, rationalization in particular. Throughout our analysis we draw upon selected themes from the show and examine them from a contemporary Weberian perspective (e.g. see Ritzer 1993).

Let us enter the parallel between *American Idol* and the American Presidential campaign from a handy trailhead. Contestants on *American Idol* are routinely asked why they want to be crowned American Idol and what being an American Idol means to them. Such questions are obviously common in American Presidential campaigns alike. Answers are similar as well. For instance, 2003 *American Idol* winner Ruben Studdard pronounced that an American Idol is "someone who represents the people" (Stahl 2004). Similarly George W. Bush ran his 2000 campaign by making himself known as "a uniter, not a divider." Also in both cases the leader—musical or administrative—is elected by the people (ironically it is worth noting that *American Idol* winners and runners-up gather significantly more votes than their political counterparts). In both cases, elected winners have a limited "term" of sorts—indicated by constitutional laws in the President's case and stipulated by the annual succession of Idol crownings in the case of the musical contest. Moreover, in both cases, winners and voters must be American—no votes or contestants coming from outside the country are accepted. And in both cases the contestants subject themselves to public scrutiny of both their public and private lives, albeit access to such information is highly controlled and scripted for strategic reasons. In addition, both *American Idol* finalists and Presidential candidates carry out public performances that betray their economic dependence on funding sponsors (e.g. Ford and Coca-Cola in the case of *American Idol*, only to mention a few).

The parallels, however, run deeper than this. Those that we have chosen to focus on in more depth are to be found in the very structure of political values that underlie both spectacles. Just like American political vision, the philosophy of *American Idol* is grounded in the *instrumental rationality* typical of an advanced market-based democratic bureaucracy. Weber (see Bendix 1977) believed there were four different ideal types of rationality: value-oriented, affective, traditional, and instrumental. Value-oriented rationality refers to conduct undertaken in light of ethical, aesthetic, religious or other types of motives that are intrinsic to behavior and not goal-driven. Affective rationality refers to action undertaken to satisfy emotional and other affective needs, drives, and wishes. Traditional rationality refers to conduct undertaken as a result of custom or habit. Finally, instrumental rationality refers to behavior enacted as means to an end, that is, to behavior as calculated pursuit.

The central characteristic of *American Idol* and the American electoral campaign is its bureaucratic, instrumental rationality. In "Politics as a Vocation," Weber (1918) defines the modern state as an entity possessing a monopoly on the legitimate use of physical force. State politics, according to Weber, translates into activities in which the state engages in order to alter the relative distribution of social power. Within such a structure, if they want to succeed at what they do, modern statesmen must look to disinterested calculation and the ability to distance themselves from the governed, rather than saintly devotion to a mission. U.S. Presidential candidates—despite their occasional rhetorical appeal to other-worldly godliness or to collective myths like the "American Dream"—know this well, but so do the architects of the success of *American Idol*. On *American Idol*, musical vocation, talent, and genius are the object of constant lip service, but in the end the true strength of the show is not musical and aesthetic but instead political and bureaucratic. The contemporary music industry—the artistic counterpart of the modern state—exercises its quasi-monopoly on the public's musical knowledge by selecting candidates for musical leadership that for the most part are not interested in taking risks. Past winners of *American Idol* are but epitomes of *McDonaldized* (Ritzer 1993) music: efficient formulas calculated to ensure predictability and control in sound and sales. Mediocrity, in a McDonaldized economy, becomes a marketing stratagem. And indeed, as the case goes in a McDonaldized market, there is no tolerance for deviations from the instrumental rational norm. Take Fantasia Barrino, for example, despite being undoubtedly the most talented winner of *American Idol* over the past five seasons (at least in Phillip's mind), her reception among audiences has been marred by her multiple stigmas as an African-American single mother (consider, for example, her song "Baby Mama," which was widely criticized for instilling poor family values in her fans).

There are three important characteristics of this instrumental rationality that we will discuss here. The first characteristic is that of *freedom of access*. Anyone in the U.S. may participate in the race to be President and to be American Idol, regardless of race, gender, class, or other *ascribed social status* (though in both cases age limitations exist). Freedom of access to both contests reveals a fundamental principle of American democracy: power and its structures are seemingly universally accessible, and anyone can become a leader by way of individual *achievement*. But herein lies also a pair of notable contradictions of the system: first, those from certain unchangeable backgrounds or in possession of certain innate qualities are more likely to win, and, second, the rewards promised to the wannabe idol or wannabe President are not limited to gratefulness for their selfless dedication to the public good (whether aesthetic or moral) as the democratic principle should have it. Instead, the rewards include personal career advancement, fame, success, power, and wealth which often turn the strategies of achievement into an instrumental pursuit. More precisely, in the case of the Presidency, the elected contestant gets to become the most powerful person in the world, whereas in *American Idol*, the winner gets a prize of one million dollars, a five-album deal with one of the parent companies of BMG—which owns Freemantle North America, the company that produces the show—and innumerable opportunities for enrichment as a celebrity endorser.

In Weberian terms, these structural conditions most often manifest themselves in instrumental—rather than affective, tradition, or valued-based—action. In spite of the show's (or the campaign's) continuous appeals to the emotional expressiveness of musical performance (or to the populist genuineness of the character), such appeals reveal the careful impression management of their personas. Such appeals are evident (and evidently demagogical and cheesy), for example, when narratives about the contenders are presented to the public in special mini-documentaries about their past—always staged in their home towns, among families and friends, and often taking place in small, "wholesome" communities where the newly famous seems always to hail from "the house next door." Common features of these documentaries are themes of "fabricated authenticity" (see Peterson 1999), "training, evaluation, work, and social advancement" that reveal the "utopian mappings of American character and opportunity structures" (Stahl 2004: 213).

Second, and obviously related to the above point, participation in the race to become either an American Idol or an American President is not only based on free access as a competitor, but also on free access as a voter. As Stahl (2004) has remarked, this is a crucial difference between, say, *American Idol* and other successful reality shows like *Big Brother* or *Survivor*. Whereas on the latter two shows contestants are kicked off weekly by members of the same cast, *American Idol* runners are voted off by "America." "America"—as contestants, judges, and Ryan Seacrest, the show's merry host, constantly refers to as their voting viewers—assumes a mystical aura in the show, almost as if she was a demi-goddess with an enlightened musical mind and artistic taste of her own but an authority coming not from tradition but populist acceptance. Any time "America" is evoked—as in "The judges loved it, but will America love it as well?" or "Vote for me, America!"—she feels more and more real and yet more and more ethereal and goddess-like at the same time. Not unlike much religious practice, her divinity works by instilling fear in her apostles. Inevitably concerned with accidentally offending her, *American Idol* singers thus avoid taking chances with original material or with performances that deviate far from the canons of shared taste.

America's mysterious but divine choices lend a certain tone of civic religiosity to the contest. The contestants come off as the chosen ones: souls blessed with musical talent and driven to work hard for the rest of their career in order to improve their talent and by doing so repay their debt to "America." It is indeed no accident that the crowned winner is but an "idol;" a figure which exacts rightful adoration, glorification, and respect from its subjects, and yet an idol which in true American fashion is ultimately the embodiment of a demagogy of common faith and collective populist will rather than traditional authority.

A third interesting political feature of the show, and the third parallel between *American Idol* and American Presidential politics, has to do with the show's ideology of meritocracy. As Weber has explained, merit-centered ideologies have taken an especially strong hold in Protestant societies because merit is a manifestation of religious devotion and self-abnegation through faith and hard work. On *American Idol*, merit is—as we have seen—determined by "America" through a process based on quasi-religious display of collective faith and will, but also through the exercise of forces more similar to the brutality of a modified social Darwinism than the grace of a musical demi-goddess. In fact, year after year, the show begins with exposure of a few musical freaks to public humiliation. This is when the slow-witted, the out-of-shape, the weird, and the uncool get their twenty-five seconds of fame/shame. The early stages of the show are interesting enough to be the subject of great curiosity. Something similar happens in Presidential campaigns. Because anyone can run, it just so happens that the majority of those who do will embarrass themselves for lacking the characteristics desired by the masses—regardless of how far-sighted, original, or courageous the poor fellows are. At this stage, public attention, in both contests, is often generated by the seeming need to humiliate and cast pity upon the sorry characters, a combination—that of pity and humiliation—typical of freak shows in America ever since Barnum's circus gained widespread popularity.

After the early rounds give way to the more competitive stages, the show's ideology of merit takes on its most obvious and also most unbecoming features. Week after week, the contestants choose and perform familiar songs on stage, parroting the conventions of well-known performers, singing styles, and musical genres. Wannabe "American Idols" are never good enough (or at least they are not allowed to be) to write and perform their own songs, and their cover-song choices are highly restricted by what the producers want "America" to hear. The singers' merit, therefore, lies in the ability to be as "bland and derivative" (Stahl 2004: 217) as the most undemanding audiences may demand. After all, the audience of *American Idol* is the widest there can be on TV; cross-cutting boundaries of age, class, gender, and race. The merit of the contestants then is connected to their ability to sing mainstream music in a mainstream fashion for a mainstream medium. If they manage to offend the least number of people during the forty-something number of marketing sessions—that is, a season's *American Idol* episodes—then they are the safe winner for an audience who is sufficiently comfortable with them by the end of the year. As in American Presidential politics, forget qualities of leadership, the winner's merit is nothing but synonymous of being the least objectionable, and we, as the audiences, have nothing but the dubious fortune of being stuck in the largest focus group in history.

COMMUNITY

Music is a form of communication. Talk surrounding musical expression is also a form of communication. Any investigation of the political significance of music must therefore consider it as a communicative exchange. In this section we discuss how the formation of polity—another word for political community—is grounded in discourse. *Discourse* is the technical term referring to the whole of communicative exchanges taking place among people, as well as to discrete instances of communication. Discourse refers to both the content of that exchange and the form in which that exchange takes place. Discourse is not only made of talk and words, but more importantly for us, also symbolic vehicles like musical sounds. Discourse *is* power; power that may repress but also power that may articulate, or in other words create, produce. Music, for example, has the power to repress communities, at least according to some sociologists as we have seen, but also the power to form them. A common example of communities formed around music is that of subcultures. The concept of subculture, or tribe, or scene,[3] refers to a network of people loosely affiliated around shared understandings, ways of communicating, and similar lifestyles. Sub-cultures/scenes/tribes include communities formed around such musical genres as jazz, punk, Indie rock, heavy metal, Riot Grrrl rock, rap, goth, and hip-hop, only to name a few.

As the various instances of musical scenes and subcultures demonstrate, communities emerge out of communicative exchanges, whether these happen at dance clubs, garages, stadiums, lounges, bars, or outdoor fields. The nature of these communities is often political in the traditional sense—as in the case of Riot Grrrl's feminist protest music—but not always necessarily so. For example, in the case of the musical TV show *Dora the Explorer*, music seems to be effective in producing both a sense of self and identity among its young fans, as well as a sense of communal inclusion—through participation—to something greater than the individual, be that family, a fan community, or society at large. Music in this sense works both as a form of knowledge that the child is in the process of acquiring, and as a form of practice in which the child (and adult alike, if one happens to be co-present) partakes. Knowing about Dora and her musical refrains, interacting with Dora herself or with others is then a form of discourse that produces the very subjects (the children) it *interpellates*—that it, is calls out—thus constituting them as members of a community. This is an example of the productive power of music.

Dora and the Constitution of Community

Dora the Explorer is an American television show featured on the U.S. children's television channel Nickelodeon. If you do not have children in your household, or if you are never near them, chances are you have never seen or heard of Dora. But the reality is quite different if little ones are in your life. Dora, chances are, inevitably *is and has been* a full member of your family ever since your child was able to focus on the TV set for more than five seconds.

Dora the Explorer was born as a pilot show in 1999 and later in 2000 it became a regular series first on the U.S. networks Nickelodeon and

---

3 These terms do not necessarily refer to the same thing. The history of "subcultural studies" has been marked by the shifting popularity of these terms. Currently scenes and tribes are preferred, as they refer to entities more complex, heterogenous, and loosely connected than the concept of subculture did.

then on CBS, the Canadian channel TreeHouse, and on CITV and Nick Jr. in the United Kingdom. Following her initial success in English, Dora has been dubbed into Spanish, French, Japanese, German, Irish, Dutch, Russian, Malay, Indonesian, Italian, and Hebrew; not too shabby for a 7-year-old explorer! Dora is also an extremely successful retail product, generating sales of all kinds— ranging from dolls and toys to clothing, media, food, and bedroom furniture.

The show's audience is composed primarily of infants, toddlers, and other pre-school-aged children and young elementary school-aged children, both girls and boys—with an apparent concentration of the former, as the market-savvy release of the boy-centered spin-off show "Go, Diego, go!" by Nickelodeon reveals. The key ingredient of Dora's recipe for success is repetition. Dora's exploring adventures are remarkably identical to one another. First, a problematic situation arises. This prompts Dora and her loyal monkey companion "Boots" to scout the surrounding area for solutions. Second, Dora needs *your* help as *you* need to guide her (by screaming at the television) through a three-leg journey. Along the journey two friends of hers always show up to help: her resource-full backpack and her know-it-all map. Third, Dora, Boots and other friends successfully complete their mission, often defeating the sneaky "Swiper the Fox" in the process. Throughout her endearing adventures Dora and companions play music, sing, dance, and regularly invite *you* to join them on the musical fun.

Dora can be quite persuasive. Throughout the show she constantly turns around to address *you*—a clear example of the sociological phenomenon known as interpellation—and to face *you*. By doing this she compels *you* to participate—whether your job is to help her by selecting one of the options laid out the screen, or by shouting out and singing and dancing along, or by sharing with her and Boots what *your* favorite part of the show was (to which, she agreeably replies: "I liked that too!"). And a lot of compelling, indeed, she does. One minute you have to spur her and Boots to jump obstacles by screaming "Salta! Salta!" ("Jump!" in Spanish) or to chase away the nefarious Swiper by yelling three times "Swiper, no Swiping!" and the next minute you find singing along "Backpack, backpack! Backpack, backpack." One minute you cannot help humming along with the "I'm the Map" refrain and the next you are driven to dancing to the tune of the victory song "Lo hicimos! We did it!" In sum, there is so much to do and so much to see, that by the end of the show you really feel like you have accomplished something together. And that is the point: watching *Dora the Explorer* is about accomplishing something together, and by doing so building community, friendship, and common values.

As John Dewey (1916: 5) explained, "Society exists not only by transmission, by communication, but it may fairly be said to exist in transmission, in communication." Following Dewey (1916) and James W. Carey (1992), we may argue that much of popular music in general, and the music featured in *Dora the Explorer* in particular, is linked to deeply significant political processes. By political here we do not refer to power distribution, legislation, jurisprudence, or governance, but rather something more fundamental: the very constitution of polity or community. In fact, by singing along with Dora and friends, children participate in the creation of a mediated form of fellowship. Members of this fellowship include significant others present in the household (e.g. parents and siblings who happen to be watching), significant others mediated by the television or musical recordings, and the generalized other (Mead 1934) embodied by some of the program's characters and actions. Association in this fellowship is based on the most quintessential attribute of community: the sharing of communicative rituals. The most prominent rituals at work here are the aural components of the show, such as the songs and the non-musical refrains (e.g. "Swiper, no swiping!") employed throughout all *Dora the Explorer* episodes. Continuous participation in the musical performances of *Dora the Explorer* results in the formation of a community across time and space, as if in an archetypal "sacred ceremony that draws persons together in fellowship and commonality" (Carey 1992: 18).

This view of music is based on the idea of communication as ritual, rather than communication as transfer of information (Carey 1992). When we understand music as ritual, we are able to conceive of music playing, dance, singing as

> [a] real symbolic order that operates to provide not information but confirmation, not to alter attitudes or change minds but to represent an underlying order of things, not to perform functions but to manifest an ongoing and fragile social process.
>
> (ibid.: 19)

Because Dora demands that *you* participate in her adventures, watching *Dora the Explorer* comes to resemble a daily ceremony marked by the sharing of a common faith or by a communion of values. Dora's incitation and admonitions to help her and friends thus constitute the building of a moral community punctuated by musical ritualistic celebrations of an "ordered, meaningful cultural world that can serve as a control and container for human action" (ibid.: 18–19). An example drawn from my (Phillip's) family life will serve to illustrate these important points. As I watch *Dora the Explorer* with my daughter, we will often exchange knowing glances at each other throughout the show as if in order to share the feeling that we both *recognize* what is going on. Little children take great pleasure in recognition; by noticing a symbol, distancing it from co-present others, and by communicating to those close to them that in fact they "know" that symbol they mark their world as a familiar one. In doing so, they also constitute a sense of self based on the very sense of habit that recognition entails and at the same time they constitute the social bonds that tie people together (Dewey 1916). Thus, by recognizing Dora and friends over repeated ritualistic encounters, and by sharing the significance of that recognition—whether through glances, attempts to hum along or utter words, or by learning lyrics and melodies by heart—a verbal and sonorous tie between people is created.

Singing with Dora is, in sum, an expression of community bonds (Turner 1975) that transcend the mediated context of television watching or record playing. Singing and dancing with Dora stands as the epitome of community formation by way of possessing things in common. These "things" include knowledge of songs and the significant symbols they are made of, shared feelings of joy in light of accomplishment ("Lo hicimos! We did it!"), determination and confidence ("Come on, vamonos, everybody let's go, come on let's get to it, I know that we can do it!"), the ability to master one's body in desirable ways (by dancing, pointing, etc.), and friendship and camaraderie ("Got a place you need to get? I can get you there, I bet. I'm the map!"). Hence, partaking in Dora's rituals by becoming one with its refrains allows children and adults alike to engage in—as Durkheim (1953: 95) would have it—a "projection of the ideals created by that community" (e.g. "Swiper, *no swiping*!").

CONCLUSION

In sum, the three contexts examined here—Constellation's political and aesthetic politics of authenticity, *American Idol's* instrumental rationality, and *Dora the Explorer* fanhood—show how music works as a technology of polity production. Music can be used to control, shape, form, and even oppress groups, thus working as an effective tool in social organization, socialization, and community formation. As these examples have shown, politics enters music—and music enters politics—in multiple ways, often radically removed from the traditional connotation of "politics and music" as protest song.

5

RACE, CLASS, AND GENDER

If asked, most sociologists would agree that the issue of social stratification lies at the very core of their research and theoretical concerns. Social stratification—the ordering of society into hierarchies of people in relation to the amount of broadly defined privileges they enjoy—is so important to sociologists because it holds the key to a better understanding, and consequently to the potential rectification, of social injustices. The study of social stratification is also important to sociologists because it deals with at least three of the most important markers of social existence: race, class, and gender.

For the most part, sociologists tend to study race, class, and gender as either causes or effects of social and cultural forces. Think, for example, about—even on the basis of anecdotal data that may be easily available to you—how variables like musical preferences, subcultural involvement, or concert attendance seem to be often related to racial, gender, or class categories. For example, we may very well observe and conclude—more or less systematically—that opera attendance is more typical amongst upper-class whites than others. Observations such as this are easy to make and difficult to refute. Yet, they often explain less than it seems. For instance, how do they explain the fact that people from other ethnic and class backgrounds enjoy going to the opera too?

In this chapter we attempt to challenge the very ideas of race, class, and gender as conventionally understood. More precisely, we believe and argue that treating race, class, and gender as "given"—that is, as characteristics that can be easily assessed along a range of discrete variables much like one would do when answering a questionnaire for a survey—and studying them as causes and effects can only tell part of a story. We suggest instead that race, class, and gender ought to be studied as intersubjective accomplishments: meaningful things that people do together (see Garfinkel 1967; West and Zimmerman 2002). By taking this approach, we obviously do not intend to deny that race, class, and gender are "real." It is obvious that they are real as it should be apparent to anyone that visible forms of discrimination, stereotyping, and disadvantage are meted out on the basis of such characteristics. Nonetheless, we intend to show that these characteristics are not as immutable as most people think and that they *become* real through social processes. By exposing the social dynamics of these processes we hope to show that the realities of race, class, and gender are contingent on social action, and thus amenable to change, to being otherwise. In doing so we hope to provide you with intellectual tools to dismantle social inequalities based on unfair categorizations of ascribed social statuses.

Social constructionists argue that reality is the emergent outcome of processes of social interaction. Social realities are dependent on such factors as language and language use, history and collective memory-making, power, the social meanings of space, as well as material social forces. Constructionists, in other words, believe that meaning—such as what it means to be a "man," to be "Asian," or to be "poor"—is achieved through the process of people communicating with one another in diverse situations. Such processes yield outcomes marked by *relatively* stable and *relatively* fixed agreed upon meanings—that is, meanings open to interpretation and to change.

We begin the chapter with an extended look at the constructionist literature on doing gender. This topic is arguably the clearest for pedagogical purposes, and it constitutes much of the background for our later discussions in this chapter. Our first example consists of a look into the phenomenon of making, being, and becoming a female pop star. Through a brief analysis of media coverage of the personal life of Jessica Simpson, we show that it is in the realms of visual language and spoken discourse that the social identities of famous women in music are made. The enormous attention that stars like Paris Hilton, Hillary Duff, and Jessica Simpson (but others could be mentioned) receive— especially in relation to their non-musical (e.g. gendered and sexual) lives—are examples of what historian and social theorist Michel Foucault (1990) called "confession" and thus reveal how gender and sex are subjects of discursive production, and thus of social interaction. Next we move to the world of contemporary mainstream hip hop music. As our illustration goes to show, hip hop fans and popular personas "do" race and class through an extremely delicate management of the impressions they convey about their personas. Yet, as we suggest, in doing so, they expose the fragility of the very concepts of race and class as fixed categories and thus posit an ironic challenge to the idea of musical authenticity and self-expression based on immutable notions of race and class. We conclude our chapter with a look into the music of Canadian "pop punk princess" Avril Lavigne . . . well, the expression isn't ours. Actually we wonder precisely whether "pop punk princess" is a double oxymoron: can punk, a class-based musical expression, be popular among all classes? By examining fan reviews of her debut CD we reflect on audience reception of class performance.

DOING GENDER

A central concern in sociology, and especially for social construction-ists, is people's talk (Garfinkel 1967). People talk in a variety of circum-stances for a variety of reasons, and in the process of talking, they often accomplish things. For example, socio-linguists have observed that cer-tain forms of talk are not only representational (i.e., about things, or in reference to things) but also performative, or in other words creative, constitutive of the social realities indicated in that very same talk. Think for example of the consequences of saying "I do" at a wedding ceremony. By saying "I do" a marriage is all of a sudden created. A common type of talk is that of giving *accounts* (Mills 1941; Scott and Lyman 1975). People routinely engage in "descriptive accountings of states of affairs to one another" says Heritage (1984: 136–137). Indeed, human beings determine their own future lines of conduct knowing that their conduct is open to such commentary and criticism. In other words, before they are about to do something, people wonder what they are going to say if they are asked to account for what they did and why.

A common context in which people account for their actions is that of confession (see Foucault 1990); during religious confessions religious followers are asked to account for what they have done wrong, to ask for forgiveness, and to express remorse. Confession must be truthful and based on values of full disclosure and trust. Within the context of religious practice, confession takes places on church grounds. Yet, within the greater context of social relations confession may take place elsewhere as well. Social theorist Michel Foucault (1990) found that confession—whether by religious followers or not—was so common that confession itself served as a model for many practices of disclosure. He further commented that certain types of actions—namely those dealing with the most private aspect of one's lives, such as intimate relationships, sexual behaviour and sexual preferences, etc.—

are especially subject to the demand for public disclosure and to being discussed ad nauseam.

Much like sex, gender, as West and Zimmerman (2002) have argued, is subject to extensive scrutiny, public talk, and stringent criteria of accountability. Gender and sex are indeed inextricable. Think, for example, of the rumor campaigns over the sexual orientation of *American Idol* runner-up Clay Aiken and N'Sync's Lance Bass—followed by heated announcements and revelations to the press. As these cases would show if we examined them in detail, by accounting for one's gender and sexuality, people reinforce and/or contribute to the changing of attitudes, beliefs, and behaviors. Indeed, we can say that gender is an interactional "doing," a reality subject to social definitions and negotiations, and a practice undertaken by individuals in the most routine interpersonal contexts of everyday life.

Garfinkel's (1967) classic analysis of gender is illustrative of these principles. Much of value to social constructionists emerged from his study of the life of Agnes, a male-to-female transsexual who had chosen to undergo sex reassignment at the age of 17. In his study, Garfinkel explained that Agnes had to re-educate herself to the gendered world in which she lived. Having lived as a male for the first seventeen years of her life, and then gradually needing to adapt to her identity as a female meant having to learn the practical methods whose knowledge and application were necessary for passing as a fully competent "normal" woman. In other words, prior to and after her surgery, Agnes "needed to display herself as a woman" and she was "obliged to analyze and figure out how to act within socially structured circumstances and conceptions of femininity" (West and Zimmerman 2002: 43) that those who are classified as women since birth learn early in their life.

Agnes's experiences showed that gender is a form of work, a social production if you will, that highlights "a complex of socially guided perceptual, interactional, and micropolitical activities" (ibid.: 42) that results in the categorization of someone as a man or a woman. Gender, therefore, is a social accomplishment, something that is transparently practiced in the presence of others, and carried out according to the social norms existent within particular social situations. Gender, in sum, is an emergent feature of the categorization of social interaction, something that comes off a situation in light of people's conceptions of what is proper and on the basis of beliefs and routine activities expected of members of a sex category. A good example of this comes from what Kessler and McKenna (1978) call the gender attribution process. These authors write about a child who, upon seeing the photograph of someone in a business suit, contends that the photographed person is "a man, because he has a pee-pee" (Kessler and McKenna

1978: 154). Obviously the child cannot see the presence of a penis, but he imputes it to the person on the basis of visual signs of known masculinity (the business attire). What this case goes to show is that gender is thus imputed, or attributed, to others on the basis of the surfaces (appearance, conduct, etc.) detectable in social interaction.

Understanding gender as something that people do allows us to conceptualize the interaction between a gendered audience and a gendered social actor as a *performance.* Because all musical expressions are based on performances, the field of popular music studies thus turns out to be a convenient one for the study of gender performance. Our precise interest in the following section is in how popular female musicians do gender in mediated situations and how mediated situations structure the gender performance of said musicians. We became interested in this after repeated observations that most media outlets seem to be less interested in musical sounds than they are in the mundane lives of musical celebrities. Take, for example, the likes of Jessica Simpson and her sister Ashlee Simpson, or Britney Spears, Hillary Duff, Jennifer Lopez, or Paris Hilton and try and reflect on when their names are mentioned. You will quickly conclude that their music seems to matter less and less and that, despite the limited coverage of their musical performances, everyone can promptly recognize the names of these celebrities, match names with their pictures, and even talk about these celebrities' sexual and relationship histories or their preferences when it comes to fashion, style, and travel. In these cases music, it seems, takes a backseat to incessant mediated exposure to their everyday routines. In this process we can see a clear example of doing gender in the mediated situation.

We find that in the process of doing gender in the mediated situation, female celebrities enact a unique type of femininity: the female pop star or prima donna—a construction similar to what Connell (1987) called emphasized femininity. In what follows we dissect some common characteristics of doing emphasized femininity in the mediated situation. Because of limited space we focus only on one celebrity, Jessica Simpson, but we believe that many of our arguments could be generalized to other popular personas.

Becoming a Prima Donna

During the 1980s, a unique musical and cultural revolution began as MTV began to bridge sound and image through the new medium of the music video (Kaplan 1987). Today, approximately two decades later neither MTV, nor its "grown-up" music television counterpart (VH1), or its Canadian cousin (Much Music), hardly shows music videos any more. Instead, today's MTV or Much Music viewer is greeted every day with endless gossip and talk, "reality shows," "interactive" television, alternative sports and freak shows, award shows, soaps, "college specials," and other non-musical productions defying easy categorization. A good recent example of this "reality turn" of MTV is represented by the reality/soap show *Newlyweds* with Nick Lachey and Jessica Simpson. On these highly mediated and scrupulously edited peeks into the ordinary lives of "hot" celebrities of the day, the stars live with cameras following their every (well, almost) move, showing them as they develop, maintain, and end relationships, debate the existential status of tuna fish in the context of a hurried lunch, and pretty themselves up for even more public appearances.

MTV is not alone in this trend, and for once it may even have failed at being the first to set it. Gossip and celebrity magazines have been around for a long time, yet what seems different about recent televised iterations of this genre is that (1) in their numerous public appearances, celebrities themselves seem to care less and less about the "official" reasons (like their artistic performances) that made them celebrities in the first place; and (2) celebrities and media seem to depend more and more on one another; thus entertainment media have all but relinquished their public role as critics, and celebrities have without reservation given more and more of their private lives to the intrusive eye of the popular media. The interaction of these two trends make for an interesting social situation, which allows us to study how media and female pop music celebrities interact with one another, and how out of their interaction there emerges (among other things) unique gender categories. Examples of these situations abound, so let us take a look at one (the case of Jessica Simpson), and reflect on its sociological relevance in the context of our discussion on gender.

Daughter of a Texan Baptist minister, Jessica Simpson's early "tryouts" in the music biz included performances with church choirs and on Christian music tours in the USA. Her entry into the pantheon of pop culture dates as far back as 1999 with the release of her album *Sweet Kisses*—featuring the platinum-selling single "I wanna love you forever." Despite a slow start, the album went on to sell about three million copies. Two years later Jessica Simpson released her second album, *Irresistible*, which proved to be irresistible "only" for about 750,000 consumers. But little did it matter at that point because Jessica had already secured herself a stable position in the eyes of the media with her reality show *Newlyweds*, chronicling the trials and tribulations of married life with heartthrob husband Nick Lachey, then lead singer of aptly named stud boy band "98 degrees." The popularity of the show was in large part due to her "Southern ingenuity," manifested through a series of much-talked-about hooplas, including her famous chicken of the sea mix-up (her confusion over whether she was eating chicken or tuna), her apparent belief that buffalo wings are made of buffalo meat, and her awkward congratulatory remark to U.S. Interior Secretary Gale Norton ("You've done a nice job decorating the White House!"). Following the popularity of her show, there came a third studio album, a Christmas album, major movie parts, product endorsements, talk show appearances, reality spin-offs, and constant presence on award shows.

Whereas Jessica Simpson's singing career has continued with ups and downs, her career as a celebrity has been truly remarkable. Her virginity claims—which she allegedly lost upon marrying Lachey—and her subsequent hypersexualized lingerie-clad appearances for Maxim have raised the eyebrows of skeptics, traditionalists, and voyeurs. Also her "dumb blonde" image has been subject of controversy; both the film critic Roger Ebert, Rolling Stone writer Rob Sheffield and the singer Pink have harshly criticized her intelligence. Magazine covers have also been busy with the never ending tale of her divorce from Lachey and her subsequent high-profile dates, as well as with carefully staged photo-ops of her charity work (a charity group providing reconstruction surgery for children with facial deformities), promotion of her dessert and beauty products line, as well as scrutiny of her waxing and waning body weight. Popularity contests (albeit seemingly friendly) with sister Ashlee Simpson have also contributed to raising both their profiles. So, what is sociologically interesting about Jessica Simpson's ways?

Contemporary sociologists argue that there are innumerable ways of doing gender, and therefore rather than "masculinity" or "femininity" we should speak of multiple *masculinities* and *femininities*. Speaking of masculinities and femininities allows us to reflect on the different performances of gender enacted in everyday life and on the different scripts available for performing gender. Instead of thinking about the sex roles of a man and a woman, therefore, we could think of gender role models available to all. Take, for example, in the context of popular music, famous women like Alanis Morissette, Bette Midler, Shania Twain, Erykah Badu, Bjork, and Bikini Kill's singer Kathleen Hanna. These women embody completely different notions of what it means to be "a woman." Of course something similar could be said for men: compare, for example, the variation across the gender styles of Clay Aiken, Jon Bon Jovi, Frank Sinatra, Nelly, Enrique Iglesias, Garth Brooks, and Tommy Lee. Obviously different "actors" and different ways of acting out gender scripts, right? The lesson that we learn here is that there are no feminine women and masculine men or unfeminine women and unmasculine women. There simply are different ways of being feminine and masculine, of being woman and being man, and being both, or neither, or some of both.

Despite the fact that there are multiple scripts available for performing one's gender, it seems that popular entertainment media (both in their magazine and television forms) are most intrigued with *very few* particular ways of doing femininity. We refer to one of these gender categories as "postmodern Prima Donna." What is a Prima Donna?

During the modern era the Prima Donna was the "first lady" of Italian opera, the leading female singer of an opera company. Legend has it that these Prime Donne were affected by the "diva complex" in that their success led them to become superficial, materialistic, vain, unpredictable, irritable, unreasonable, egotistical, obsessed with their own fame, and narcissistic. Today's (postmodern) Prime Donne are seemingly a bit different, judging of course from the public personas they display. While they maintain some of the characteristics of their earlier and modern counterparts, they also tend to resemble what Connell (1987) has called *emphasized femininity* and to embrace some of the traits that some theorists have found to be common in our contemporary, postmodern culture. Emphasized femininity rediscovers traditional (read: conservative) ways of being a woman in a retro fashion. This way of doing femininity entails "compliance, nurturance, and empathy" (ibid.: 187–188) and is linked with the traditional realms of the home and the bedroom. Emphasized femininity scripts demand that a woman be at peace with accommodating the desires of men and that she draw much of her sense of worth from being popular among them.

Yet, contemporary emphasized femininity also draws from more contemporary scripts. A contemporary Prima Donna blurs diverse traits by borrowing from an earlier style and recycling it in the context of the times, marked by a culture of endless superficial appearances and mediated imagery. Today's postmodern Prime Donne then are a unique mix of "diva" and "girl next door," of princess and pauper, of cosmopolitan jet setter and wholesome small town girl, of hypersexualized seductress and virgin. This formula for performing gender is often applied today by several pop music stars (e.g. Britney Spears, Hillary Duff, etc.) and by the media outlets which broadcast their performances. Being a postmodern Prima Donna is therefore both about celebrities acting this way to be easily recognized and about media framing their public personas in this fashion to feed audiences' expectations. Being a postmodern Prima Donna is a complex mediated act of gender construction.

Acting like a Prima Donna entails, for example, regular acts of public confession to the media. Celebrity confessions are incredibly extensive these days. Anyone with media access can easily find what Jessica likes to eat, how she likes to decorate the table, that she is in the midst of considering adoptions, and that she has had fantasies about Brad Pitt, and more. Her private life, because of her continuous confessions, is constantly public and neither she nor her publicists seem to mind.

In confessing with regularity and depth, Prime Donne like Jessica Simpson blur the distance between private and public spaces. A pair of concepts often used by sociologists, that of *private and public spheres*, help us understand Prime Donne's performance of gender a bit better. Traditionally, sociologists explain, men's domain has been in the public sphere—for example, in the work of paid employment, politics, and so forth. Women's activities and identities, instead, have been for the most part focused around the home, where "labor of love" activities such as child-rearing, relationship maintenance, and housework are meant to take place. Of course, these boundaries have become blurred over time, yet sociologists find with great regularity examples of women being pulled back (or pushing themselves back) in the private sphere. For example, when musicians become famous, most mass media continuously attempt to uncover their "private" lives, thus incidentally confining them again to the private sphere of childrearing, home-making, and relationships. Jessica Simpson's own reality shows—staged in the context of her home—functions in this sense as a return to the private sphere. Beside the mentioned reality show, public attention to Simpson constantly focuses on her dating adventures, struggles with divorce, with her body shape, and family life. Her own presentation of self in the context of children's charity work, adoption plans, promotion of both beauty and food products also continue to highlight her emphasized femininity. To boot, her small town ingenuity and naïveté, traditional moral values, and emotional ups and downs mark her emphasized femininity as a particularly histrionic one, punctually combined with her image as a demure yet glamorous, successful, vain, hypersexualized diva.

Confession, according to Foucault, does not uncover a pre-existing reality, but instead makes one anew. Thus, in being a consistent player in public discourse, or in other words in constantly generating talk about their private lives, postmodern Prime Donne like Jessica Simpson can never logically lament "unfair media representation." The media are hardly *re-presenting* these women, since any trace of their livelihood *outside* of the media's eye seems to exist. Rather than media representation of a pre-existing reality then, this is case of actual social *construction of meaning* in the mediated situation. Therefore, as West and Zimmerman (2002: 42) explain, their Prima Donna persona is best understood as a "situated doing, carried out in the virtual or real presence of others . . . as both an outcome and a rationale" for their actions.

Being and becoming a Prima Donna demands careful efforts. Agnes, whom Garfinkel studied, did everything she could to pass for a "normal woman." Prime Donne like Jessica Simpson need to do everything they can to pass for diva-like "emphasized" women: star-like-women who do what some others only wish they could do, including being beautiful and glamorous, talented, popular, successful, famous, graceful, and enjoying romance, yet all of it mixed with a certain grounding in conservative ideals like selflessness, sacrifice, ingenuity, innocence, willingness to stick it out during hardship, etc. Acting like a Prima Donna is—to borrow again from Garfinkel's (1967: 129) analysis of Agnes—attempting to be "120 per cent female," that is, managing to conduct herself appropriately in the most mundane occasions in order to be accountable as "normal" as the girl next door (with the same wishes, hopes fears, misfortunes, limitations, etc.) and yet as "special" as the downtown girl (with the ability to make dreams and hopes come true, fearless, famed, and free, and yet at times nostalgically longing for a simpler lifestyle).

In conclusion, the media—as important social agents in our post-modern times—play an obvious role in setting the parameters of what constitutes normal and expected gendered behaviour, for women much more stringently than for men. Doing gender in the mediated situation is therefore as much about "doing" gender as it is about "being done" by available gender categories and preferred media casts. The activity of doing gender in the mediated situation is thus hardly free from restrictions. It is hardly possible for someone to plan in advance what type of gender performances one will engage in for the next five or ten years and then freely execute that plan. Even trend-setters like Madonna who have wished to play by their own rules have often collided with insurmountable walls of expectations. Chipping away at that wall, if one wishes to build new roles, is, however, an act which shows both courage and promise.

DOING RACE: PERFORMING THE WIGGER

Despite the fact that is has now been in use for about ten years, the term "wigger"—or the accent-inflected spelling "wigga"—is absent from most English language dictionaries. Yet, ask any 10–18-year old in North America to give you a definition and chances are that you will hear a similar answer: "a wigger is a white man or woman who acts like a black man or woman." The Internet-based encyclopedia Wikipedia similarly defines a wigger as a "white person who emulates phrases, mannerisms, and fashions commonly and stereotypically associated with black people or hip hop cultures" (http://en.wikipedia.org/wiki/Wigger). The term is a slang expression combining "w"—the initial of "white" or "wannabe"—and "-igger," from the highly derogatory word "nigger." Similar combinations are known among youths, such as "migger" and "chigger"—respectively indicating a Mexican and/or a Muslim and/or a Middle Eastern, and a Chinese man heavily involved into the hip hop scene, and obviously "acting black." While all these words are likely to offend some, leave others perplexed or neutral and even evoke a sense of pride among those who embrace the label, the recent success of characters like "Ali G"—impersonated by British comedian Sacha Baron Cohen—clearly testifies to the fact that "wiggers" have become more highly visible than ever in popular culture and the media and that a sociological understanding of this phenomenon is badly needed.

From a historical perspective, there is nothing new with the phenomenon of people from different ethnic backgrounds adopting the subculture of people from other ethnic backgrounds. For example, white people have mimicked black people's music-centered subcultural behaviors and taste throughout the twentieth century. In the 1920s and 1930s, the White Negroes, in the 1930s and 1940s, the Zoot Suiters and later hipsters, in the 1950s, the beatniks, and in the 1960s and 1970s, the mods have all been believed to be imitating the mannerisms and fashion of Black Americans or Black Britons of the times. Various scholars might remark that these and similar phenomena constitute examples of *cultural appropriation*: attempts by one person or group belonging to one culture or subculture to co-opt a style that originated among people of a different culture or subculture. Cultural appropriation, or *co-optation*, has been subject to a great deal of condemnation in popular culture studies. Most scholars and observers agree that co-optation is a reflection of the commercialization of culture, the commodification of style and identity, and the disrespect that some social agents pay toward values such as originality, individuality, and unique style. But whereas cultural appropriation arguments are generally very useful for understanding "why" co-optation occurs, in this chapter we are more interested in explaining "how" such phenomena occur, especially at the level of mundane practice.

Following our analysis of the personal life of Jessica Simpson in light of her gender performance, in what follows we extend our constructionist performative argument to the case of race. From this perspective we view "wiggers" as social agents engaged in the presentation of self and identity in everyday life. Studying "wiggers" highlights how race is performed through impression management, and how appearances of the racialized self may be successful (that is, convincing) or unsuccessful on the basis of both categorizations by audiences of their performances and on the basis of the very qualities of those performances. To assist us in this endeavor we draw upon the *dramaturgy* of Erving Goffman (1959). Goffman's dramaturgic study of everyday life employs a view of social interaction as drama. From this perspective, individual and collective expression is understood as carefully—albeit at times involuntarily—managed self-expressive action and impression-making.

Studying the dramaturgic performance of a wigger identity is an exercise in observing the effectiveness of a role performance. When a role is performed well, the person who performs it will be accorded respect and admiration. When a role is not performed well, the actor may be subject to ridicule and stigma. It is important to highlight what this type of study can achieve. By interpreting this approach incorrectly one could end up suggesting that race is nothing but a form of empty play and that therefore anyone may freely *choose* the racial or ethnic category to which one wishes to belong and, upon acting the part right, successfully gain that social identity. Such an interpretation would be nonsense. Ethnic categories are often created on the basis of racialized appearances, and for all one may "do" on an interaction stage, one's claims will still be subject to scrutiny and categorization by scrupulous audiences. Yet, this is precisely the point we wish to emphasize: race is meaningful only insofar as people direct their attention to it as a significant symbol, and thus engage in the interpretation of its meanings on the basis of role performances. The potential of the constructionist approach in the realm of studies of race is in fact its aptness at discovering how racial appearances and role performances come to *pass* and thus become institutionalized and taken for granted.

Let us begin with a close observation of what wiggers may do. A popular humorous website on "wiggers" (wiggaz.com) provides us with a nice insight into the typical behavior and appearance of a "wigger": a "wigga" must be fly, must listen to rap/hip hop, and must dress in "wigger gear." This handy definition holds to key to the "wigger's" presentation of self as it highlights its three central dimensions: character, taste, and appearance. Let us examine these in order.

A "wigger's" character, as we learned, must be "fly." The online "Urban Dictionary"—extremely useful for all slang expressions—succinctly defines "fly" as cool and in style. Coolness, as conceptualized by dramaturgist sociologists Lyman and Scott (1970: 145) refers "to the capacity to execute physical acts, including conversation, in a concerted, smooth, self-controlled fashion in risky situations, or to maintain affective detachment during the course of encounters involving considerable emotion." Being cool, therefore, is about "keeping one's cool" in situations where poise may be under pressure. Lyman and Scott (ibid.: 145–146) assert that losing one's cool holds physical risk (as in getting beat up), financial risk, and social risk. Social risks are of particular interest here, as they may arise just about any time people interact with one another.

The most common social risk that "wiggers" may perceive is that of being exposed to others for what they "really are" and thus ridiculed for alleged lack of originality or authenticity. Yet, and this is important, "wiggers" are not *automatically* reprimanded in all social interactions by all people, indeed there are situations in which an individual performing a "wigger" persona and claiming a "wigger" identity may be accepted by others. Such acceptance reveals an interesting phenomenon, especially when it occurs in the context of inter-racial relationships. When an actor's claim to a particular subcultural identity closely tied to ethnic markers is accepted, *ethnic identity* is "made." This goes to show that ethnic social identity is based on both performance (what the actor does) and categorization (the audience's response). When, as in the case of "wiggers," an actor's visible racial traits (i.e. skin color) do not correspond to the racial traits typical of the ethnic identity into which he/she wants to be categorized, and despite this claim he/she is still successful, we can say that ethnicity itself is being "done" in open disregard of the obtrusive markers of race.

A pair of examples ought to simplify this considerably. Let us examine first Eminem and later Fergie. Eminem—born Marshall Mathers—is a 34-year-old white rapper from Detroit whose enormous success as a rapper and hip-hopper has undoubtedly been facilitated by his coolness—some might suggest—in an art world dominated by African-American performers. Eminem's coolness (again, for at least some of his audiences) comes from the aplomb with which he has handled numerous scandalous situations in which he has been involved. Whether he has been accused of misogyny, homophobia, hatred for the U.S. President or for other rappers, Eminem has always parlayed accusations into claims of his authenticity as a straight-talking, driven, tough-skinned, self-made-from-the-'hood rapper. His coolness has allowed him to expand his audience by crossing racial, age, class, and gender boundaries. Furthermore, his coolness of character has highlighted his singing abilities and musical skills. His talent for alliteration, assonance, and his ability to change both tone of voice and rhythm with ease even within the same tune have garnered him levels of credibility unprecedented for white rappers. As Lyman and Scott (1970: 151) remarked, "tests of coolness" such as "highly stylized dialog of insult" (traditionally, rap *is* a form of dialog) and self-aggrandizement require the effective mobilization and control of material and symbolic objects and forces.

The second normative characteristic of a "wigger" is that he/she listens to hip hop or rap. This is an essential component of the social identity of the wigger. Hip hop and rap are the two most popular musical expressions of black youths today. From a dramaturgist perspective hip hop music functions as a "prop" supporting the staging of the wigger persona. Remember that for Goffman presentation of the self is understood from a theatrical metaphor: individuals wear masks to project a particular image to an audience. In doing so on stage—that is, in front of others—they follow scripts, manipulate the setting where they stage their performances, and within their role they perform what is expected of them by their audiences, that is, they act out a line to protect their front. Hip hop music works as a prop in the sense that it enables the performer to convey a convincing expression of self. Listening is a private activity but private listening does not have much potential for conveying social meanings. Listening to music is then turned into a prop for a social performance whereby the listener becomes an actor publicly staging his or her performances before an audience. "Wiggers' " public acts of listening, as conspicuous displays of their taste, take well-known forms: walking on public sidewalks while carrying "ghetto-blasters," wearing oversized headphones that only in part muffle loud music sound, driving low-rider or "pimp" automobiles turned into bass cars, and more.

Listening publicly to rap clearly demonstrates subcultural involvement and identity, but it does not do so as clearly as *performing* music. "Wiggers," much like rappers, will then often turn everyday conversation settings into improvised rap sessions and rhyme contests. Doing so, the point goes, constitutes a way through which claims to ethnic social identities can be successfully achieved. In other words, music in this case turns into an instrumental tool utilized by people to manage impressions, manipulate realities, and achieve their social aims. Doing race in "the wigger way" thus primarily entails a set of staging techniques and props whose meanings are socially variable, rather than fixed racial traits.

Being in style is a necessary component of this process. Style entails aspects of consuming behavior that we examine elsewhere in this book. Style is a form of conspicuous consumption of taste and a strategy for the performance of identity, but it is also a racialized performance that not only refers to clothing and body-adornment but to an entire ensemble of signs that work by staging and sustaining the difference of social actors from others. Try, for instance, to compare the style—not the fashion sense but the signing style—of Jessica Simpson with that of

Black Eyed Peas' singer Fergie. In her album *Sweet Kisses*, Jessica Simpson sings a song entitled "Heart of Innocence." An excerpt from the lyrics reiterates some of the points made earlier in this chapter about her presumed virginity and related gender performance:

> Sometimes I wake up in the dark of night
> And in my mind there's a picture of you
> I know someday this dream will come alive
> So for now your shadow will do
> I've never seen your face
> But I know your in my heart
> Maybe someday some place
> I'll hold you in my arms
> I have a gift for you
> Something that I've held on to
> Waiting for your sweet caress
> No ribbon has been untied
> From all that I hold inside
> And only you will possess
> This heart of innocence . . .

In contrast, take the more aggressive, urban, overtly seductive, and in-charge "street-like" style of Fergie. Consider, for example, the song "My Humps" from the Black Eyed Peas' album *Monkey Business*. Addressing Will.I.am, who inquires what she intends on doing with all that junk that she seemingly has inside her trunk, she responds:

> I'ma get, get, get, get, you drunk,
> Get you love drunk off my hump.
> My hump, my hump, my hump, my hump, my hump,
> My hump, my hump, my hump, my lovely little lumps
> > (Check it out)
>
> I drive these brothers crazy,
> I do it on the daily,
> They treat me really nicely,
> They buy me all these ices.
> Dolce & Gabbana,
> Fendi and NaDonna
> Karan, they be sharin'
> All their money got me wearin' fly
> Brother I ain't askin,
> They say they love my ass 'n,
> Seven Jeans, True Religion's,
> I say no, but they keep givin'
> So I keep on takin'

And no I ain't taken
We can keep on datin'
I keep on demonstrating.
My love (love), my love, my love, my love (love)
You love my lady lumps (love),
My hump, my hump, my hump (love) . . .

By borrowing from hip hop imagery and iconic behaviors, by using African American slang, and by directly engaging a black man, Will.I.am, on stage, Fergie performs a style of racialized femininity typical, *arguably*, of *some* young urban African-American women and crosses racial boundaries, perhaps—in the eyes of some—attempting to pass as a black persona. Or does she? As an audience member you have an important say in all of this . . .

DOING CLASS: IS AVRIL LAVIGNE PUNK?

We conclude our constructionist reflection on race, gender, and class with an analysis of the class-based performance of Canadian rocker Avril Lavigne. Avril Lavigne reached stardom in the spring of 2002, when she made her debut with the incredibly successful CD titled *Let Go*. In addition to her catchy "pop-punk" hooks, Avril caught the world of pop music by storm with what at the time seemed like an anti-Britney Spears formula of skateboarder looks, street attitude, and dark appeal. *Let Go*, and especially her single "Complicated" reached the top of the Billboard charts, gained nominations for Best Pop New Artist and Best Pop Female Artist at the 2002 Billboard Music Awards, received five Grammy nominations, and won the Best Song, Best CD, Best Female Artist, and Best Homework Song at the 2002 Radio Disney Music Awards, as well as the MTV Video Music Award for best new artist in a video. *Let Go* also went platinum on July 12, 2002, breaking record for short-time increases in sales and radio spins. By the time of writing, the album had sold over fifteen million copies worldwide. Media appearances, endorsements, endless play of her videos, and celebrity gossip have now made Avril Lavigne one of the more successful female singers of the decade. Avril Lavigne's persona, especially at the time of her debut, is our object of interest here.

In examining Avril Lavigne as we have done with Jessica Simpson, Eminem, and Fergie, we are not concerned with her self or personal identity. Instead we are interested in her public persona, in other words, with her public image and with the discourses surrounding her mediated presentation of self. By studying her self-presentation through the mass media as a complex and multifaceted performance, and by focusing on how she "does" class, we are interested in questioning how she stages her front before her audiences through the management of her style, physical appearance, life story, career, her status as a celebrity, her song lyrics, and even more. So far in this chapter we have examined elements of performance of race and gender without giving too much consideration to how audiences interpret performances. Whereas in the case of Fergie we left it up to you to discuss the contours of her performance, now we take it upon ourselves to observe how fans of Avril Lavigne's, as well as non-fans, deconstruct the credibility of her self-presentation. Our data consist of reviews of *Let Go* voluntarily submitted to various websites by internet users. Using a socio-semiotic frame of analysis, we focus on how audiences interpret the authenticity of Avril Lavigne's performance of class.

As an analytical tool we can divide audiences' readings of her CD and her persona into two broad categories: the category of *hegemonic readings* and that of *counter-hegemonic readings*. The former category includes readings *preferred* by a performer. For example, when a teacher delivers a lecture in a classroom she hopes that her students will buy into her argument without challenging her too much. A politician will have the same attitude toward a speech, a parent toward a lesson imparted to his children, and so forth. Hegemonic readings of Avril Lavigne's performances reveal that what she intended to communicate went over well with some fans:

> Hey, I wish people would stop saying such bad stuff about Avril! So she's a punk. So? Get over it! That's how she likes to express herself. Not everyone likes to be the same as everyone else.

> Yeah she's punky and I hope she puts more songs out. If you like Avril, then get the CD! I am hooked on it! Get it! You will be satisfied with your purchase. She wrote all her songs AND plays her own music. She is so good! You all really need to try this CD out. I am so glad I did!

Punk music is the soundtrack of autonomy, independence, and rebellion. As we explain elsewhere in this book, these traits are often associated with the ideal of authenticity. Authenticity is not only a moral and aesthetic value but also something which must be concretely performed, which must be "done." When audiences believe in the sincerity of a performer and in the originality and authenticity of musical expression, a performer—regardless of how actually sincere he/she may be—has managed to convey his/her front and preferred persona well. Avril's persona—at least at the time of her debut—revolved critically around stories told about her start in the musical world. Avril rebelliously dropped out of high school when she was 16 to follow her dream of becoming a singer. Her independence from social constraints continued to mark her biography and career: Avril was believed to be uncompromising on how her records were to be produced, what her image was, and what she wanted her lyrics to communicate. Compared to the likes of Christina Aguilera, Mandy Moore, and Britney Spears, her audiences found her to be low maintenance, unpretentious and down to earth, and unaffected by her celebrity status. Her looks seemingly embodied this. Avril (and her fans) were often seen wearing work shirts and rebelliously loose neck ties—a true punk uniform of sorts, a sign which expresses at once affiliation with working-class fashion and condemnation of middle and executive or debutante class respectability.

However, what works with some audiences does not work with others. Counter-hegemonic readings of Avril Lavigne's persona point to her insincerity and manufactured authenticity. These readings can be called *oppositional*. Particularly jarring to some audiences are her inconsistencies; definitive give-aways of what seems like an attempt to commodify authenticity:

Avril Lavigne is a pop singer feeding off the new punk trend. Apparently she (along with all her fans) missed the bulletin notifying those of us whose minds aren't quite as impressionable that dressing in every article of clothing ever put out by Hot Topic does not make you punk. Yet the brainless youth of America continues to eat it up, as they do with anything and everything they're spoon-fed by the media, Top 40 radio, and the sadistic, brainwashing, greedy trend whores better known as MTV executives. In July 14's August issue, Avril explained her songwriting process. "Once I sit down with the guitar, I write about what I'm feeling that day." However, in the July 1st edition of *Time* magazine, Ms. Lavigne admitted, "I sit down with a guitar player usually." Which is it, Avril? Furthermore, a look at the songwriting credits on her CD will reveal that each song was co-written with a multitude of professional songwriters. One can't help but wonder just how much of these songs was written by Avril. Yet in that same J-14 article, she claimed, "I wrote all those songs when I was sixteen." Avril is being touted as some guitar-playing, songwriting prodigy when, in reality, she's not the only force behind those tracks. But that's what sells, so I guess that makes it alright to lie, exaggerate, and present yourself as some virtuoso. Oh, and here's a bright idea for Avril to prove how punk she is. Let's have her RAP in a song. Because, ya know, most punk bands always include a rap bit or two in their songs. She's a constant contradiction. She skateboards in the video, poses for publicity shots with the board, tells YM magazine that she's good at it. Yet, in an interview with MTV, she discussed how the director of the "Complicated" video wanted her to skate in it. Ms. Tony Hawk protested, "No, dude, I suck!" One look through any teen magazine will reveal models dressed in clothing just like hers. And let's not forget the fake tattoos she wears on her arms. Because that's like ya know, sooo totally hardcore. Let me go draw a big skull and crossbones on my arm so that I can be punk too. Please. Avril Lavigne just seems fake, plain and simple.

(Review by Jessica Zietz at
http://recroommagazine.com/framesmain.htm)

Punk is first and foremost a class movement and ideology (Hebdige 1979). Its roots are to be found in working-class youth and in their alienation from a political and economic system which—these youth feel—commodifies all individual expressions. Punk is also an aesthetic ideology of sorts. Its raw sound is virtue made out of necessity: studio production, good instruments, and music lessons are expensive, unaffordable, and thus deemed undesirable. Punk is therefore rough, all but pretty, gritty, and uninterested in pretentiousness. For some audiences, therefore "to call her punk is to tarnish the images of actual punk artists and their contributions to music as a whole. Please, people, stop listening to this CD, stop wearing socks on your arms, get some real music." And:

> If you like mass manufactured entertainment, bully for you. I see no evidence of artistic merit in this collection of highly produced boring scrap. This is perfect music for supermarkets, dentist offices, and airplanes. Sure, she's cute, all dressed in her department store, suburban mall-punk duds. And, by the way, when did pop drivel earn the title of "Punk"? I know I'm getting old, but did I miss something? Punk was something different when I was younger (Stooges, NY Dolls, DK, pre-Rollins Black Flag, even the Ramones and early Clash, etc). In fact, punk was the diametric opposite of everything present in Ms. Lavigne's carefully exploited image.
>
> (Review at http://www.amazon.com)

By pointing out attempts at the commodification of punk these writers resist the co-optation of class and class-based aesthetics and ideology. What these examples go to show is that impression management does not always work. Despite how well a person may play a role, certain audiences will at times remain skeptical and challenge the sincerity and authenticity of performances. This does not take away from the notion that class is something that is performed, however. In fact and interestingly enough, in publicly rejecting the sincerity and credibility of Avril Lavigne's performance these internet users reassert the significance of performing class in certain ways and not in others. Furthermore, in doing so they too perform class, don't they?

CONCLUSION

What we have attempted to demonstrate in this chapter is that race, class, and gender are not fixed categories. In certain situations in social interaction these important markers of individual existence may look and feel as if they are unchangeable but to think of them as unchangeable does little for a critical sociological cause keen on the eradication of social injustice based on ascribed social status and qualities. If we take race, class, and gender as performances, that is, as something that people do, we enable ourselves to think in alternative ways and to reflect on how things could be otherwise. Conceptualizing race, class, and gender as performatives further allows us to reflect on social interaction, rather than on biology, as the site where social realities are created, communicated, and interpreted.

6

THE SELF AND THE LIFE COURSE

The notion of *life course* is important to a particularly sociological perspective on people and their behavior. In general, sociologists believe that people are only partially shaped by their biological and genetic capacities. Instead, our self and how we approach social life are constantly shaped by events and experiences that happen all the way through life. We change constantly if not occasionally dramatically. The concept of *life course* holds that socialization is a lifelong process (Furstenberg 2003). Accordingly, our appreciation for and use of popular music are a dynamic process that does not end when we become adults.

Social scientists have traditionally focused on popular music experiences among young audiences. The focus has been on pop music specifically as a feature of adolescent culture and, therefore, of teenagers' everyday life experiences. As Simon Frith (1981) noted in his famous sociological text, *Sound Effects*, rock music has been fundamental to the experience of growing up ever since the end of World War II. Similarly, sociologists have demonstrated increasing interest over the years in rock and pop music as an indicator of dramatic changes occurring in the social and cultural worlds of teenagers. We can trace this interest at least as far back as David Riesman's (1950) classic examination of the emergence of the *other-directed* personality in post-WWII American society. The new middle class was marked by a weakening of parental control, a preoccupation with consumption, and a shift in the meaning of leisure resulting in the masses—the lonely crowd—desperately trying to have fun. The time was ripe for the emergence of a youth culture defined by what have come to be known as pop and rock music.

The popular music industry that drives rock and pop continues to expand dramatically—beyond multi-billion dollar annual sales, globalization, CDs, MP3 technology, and the internet. Yet, lay and scholarly observers have generally ignored or underplayed an important element of social and cultural change: rock and pop are no longer limited to, nor solely the possession of, teenagers. The original generation of rock fans—the baby boomers—are now parents and, in some cases, grandparents. The music and musical culture they grew up with has stayed with them, becoming the soundtrack of North American cultures.

The aim of this chapter is to survey the many ways rock and pop pervade the everyday lives of adults in North American society. In commonsense terms, we examine what happened to the first, complete generation of rock fans: the baby boomer generation now in late middle age. We argue that rock 'n' roll music continues to serve as a critical meaning resource for its adult fans as they continuously experience the becoming of self throughout life. To better understand how music works throughout the life course we begin by discussing in some depth the concepts of self, identity, and the life course itself.

SELF, IDENTITY, AND THE LIFE COURSE

The self is probably the most important concept for all qualitative sociologists. Yet, it is often used improperly or confused with the concept of identity. Before we proceed to examine the empirical material unique to this chapter, let us discuss in some detail these important ideas. And let us begin with the self. The self, as the word itself suggests, is a reflexive object. Think, for example, of its common use in expressions like: "I hurt myself." When you hurt yourself you direct attention (the realization that you are in pain) to you as an object. In doing so you are both a subject (knower and feeler, in this case) of your action, and an object (known and felt). You are a subject in the sense that you are the one who is mustering attention and directing focus, and you are an object in the sense that such attention is focused on you. In doing so, George Herbert Mead (1934) tells us, you are *minding* yourself. It is by minding that indeed we create a sense of self. We mind our self into being by, for example, engaging in internal conversations (e.g. thinking about oneself), monitoring our sensations, experiencing feelings about the self, and so forth. The "doing" of all these things is the "doing" of the self. The self, in other words, is a constant process, a way of "selfing" ourselves into being as a result of our actions as a subject (the "I"), and as an object of our actions (the "me").

Identity refers to something different. An identity is a typification of self, either imposed upon an individual by others (*social identity*) or adopted by self (*personal identity*). For example, if others view me as a punk rocker and treat me as such, my social identity is that, indeed, of a punk rocker. Others could treat me as a punk rocker even in spite of the fact that I carefully distinguish my identity among available punk styles (and identities) and identify myself as a hardcore punk rocker (my personal identity). An identity can be more or less stable across social settings. For example, my youth friends may have always identified me as punk rocker for all my life, but if one evening I were to attend a grindcore concert and enjoy it, I may very well, at least for that evening, identify myself as (and be identified by other concert attendants as) a grindcore fan. We can refer to these momentary identities that we take up and shed on a regular daily basis as *situational identities*. So, for example, despite our more enduring social and personal identities, on any given day we can have situational identities such as bus-rider, grocery-shopper, pedestrian, etc.

The discussion above highlights the processual nature of self and identity. Think of the self as a molecule of water. A molecule of water is made up of two components: hydrogen and oxygen. A self is similarly the result of the combination of two components: the "I" and the "me." A molecule of water is always in flux throughout its life. When suspended amidst clouds and then falling from the sky, it assumes the identity of a rain drop; when frozen up high in the mountains, it has the identity of an ice crystal; when melting and flowing down the mountain, it has the identity of river water; and when merging with the ocean, it assumes the identity of sea water. Now, of course a molecule of water has no reflexivity (and no personal identity), but from this example you can at least see that its life is a never-ending process and that throughout this process it assumes different identities in light of the settings it inhabits. The same can be said of the self: throughout the life course an individual assumes different social, situational (and also personal) identities as a result of the fluidity of life and the social "pools" with which we come into contact. To the concept of the life course we now turn.

A *life course* is a patterned temporal trajectory of individual experiences. Some scholars, notably social psychologists and psychologists, like to identify objective and universal stages typical for all individuals. Interactionists and constructionists are instead less interested in determining fixed stages and more in examining how individuals assign meanings to their progression through life. In the words of Clair, Karp, and Yoels (1993: vii) their focus is more precisely on "how persons occupying different locations in social space interpret and respond to repeated social messages about the meanings of age." Reflecting on the contribution of these authors, in an influential overview of the concept and research on the life course sociologists Holstein and Gubrium (2003: 836) write:

> (1) age and life stages, like any temporal categories, can carry multiple meanings; (2) those meanings emerge from social interaction; and (3) the meanings of age and the course of life are refined and reinterpreted in light of the prevailing social definitions of situations that bear on experience through time.

As you can obviously see, the life course is therefore about the becoming of self: the fluid process through which we acquire new and diverse roles, social identities, and personal identities. Music, we argue, provides a set or symbolic resources for the definition and reinterpretation of these identities: through music we continuously self ourselves into being. But, how, precisely, do we do so?

THE BECOMING OF SELF

The existential sociological concept of *the becoming of self* is a useful guide in seeking the sociological answers to this question. Existential social thought is heavily derived from and very close in nature to symbolic interactionism. A difference is that existential sociology views the self: "as a unique experience of being within the context of contemporary social conditions, an experience most notably marked by an incessant sense of becoming and an active participation in social change" (Kotarba 1984: 223). The incessant sense of becoming is a reflection of the contemporary need for the individual to be prepared to reshape meanings of self in response to the dictates of a rapidly changing social world. The well-integrated self accepts the reality of change and welcomes new ideas, new experiences, and reformulations of old ideas and experiences that help one adapt to change (Kotarba 1987).

The idea of *becoming* is one of the most important ideas in existentialist thought across disciplines because it places responsibility for fashioning a self on the individual. Whereas Jean-Paul Sartre (1945) argued dramatically that we are condemned to be free and to choose who we are to become, Maurice Merleau-Ponty (1962) insisted more moderately and sociologically that we must ground our becoming-of-self in the real world in order to cope effectively with it. Thus, an effective strategy for becoming begins with a foundation of personal experience and the constraints of social structure, while evolving in terms of the resources presented by culture. We argue that middle-aged

North Americans work with a self built to some degree on the meanings provided by the rock 'n' roll idiom, and they continue to nurture the self within the ever-present cultural context of rock 'n' roll.

Douglas (1984) notes that there are, in fact, two analytically distinct stages of becoming-of-self with which the modern actor contends. The first is *the need to eliminate or control threats to the basic security of self* (e.g., meaninglessness, isolation from others, shame, death). Although existential psychotherapists like Yalom (1980) argue that chronic insecurity—or neurosis—is pervasive in our society, Douglas argues sociologically that it is more common for the sense of security to vary biographically, situationally, and developmentally. In general, adults try to shape everyday life experiences in order to avoid basic threats to the self. Basic threats to the adult self in our society would include divorce, the loss of a job, the loss of children (e.g., the empty nest syndrome), illness, disability, and poverty. The second stage of becoming-of-self involves *growth of the sense of self.* Growth occurs when the individual seeks new experiences as media for innovative and potentially rewarding meanings for self (Kotarba 1987). It is through growth, or self-actualization as it is often referred to today, that life becomes rich, rewarding, full, and manageable.

Accordingly, adult fans nurture their interest in and experience with rock 'n' roll music for two reasons. On the one hand, keeping up with the music and the culture that were so important to them when growing up helps them maintain *continuity* with the past and thus solidifies the sense of self security. On the other hand, working hard to keep rock 'n' roll current and relevant to their lives helps adults grow as parents, as spiritual beings, and as friends.

The concept of the *existential self* tells us that the experience of individuality is never complete; the answer to the question "who am I?" is always tentative. In the postmodern world, the mass media—including popular music—serve as increasingly important audiences to the self. The *self* is situational and mutable (Zurcher 1977). One can be various selves as the fast-paced, ever-changing, uncertain postmodern society requires. In the remainder of this chapter, we provide a working inventory of the various ways adults self themselves into being. These are experiences of self common in everyday life, closely related to roles and social and personal identities, and predicated by or embedded in rock 'n' roll culture.

The E-Self

As the rock 'n' roll fan ages, many of the attractive aspects of the earlier self become increasingly difficult to maintain. There is a tendency for youthfulness, energy, risk-taking, appearance, sensuality, and other aspects of the adolescent or young-adult self to become either less available or less desirable. Our culture does, however, provide the resource of an image of social identity that resonates with the affluence of middle age, as well as with the continuing need to establish status/ self-esteem. The *e-self* (or electronic self) refers to an experience of individuality in which the affective and philosophical self-resources of rock 'n' roll media are displaced or at least supplemented by the increasingly technological and commodified aspects of the media. For the middle-aged fan, what you play your music on can be at least as, if not more, important than what you play.

Middle age results in less concert attendance and more music experience in the comfort of home, automobile and, for the energetic, on the jogging trail. A quick reading of *Wired* magazine (October 2004), which is geared toward the affluent and technologically-interested middle-aged person, discloses the strategy of marketing rock 'n' roll to its audience. There are ads for sophisticated cell phones that allow the consumer to "keep rockin' with your favorite MP3s." The promotion for "THEWIREDAUCTION," on eBay which benefits a children's foundation, includes a "limited edition series precision bass guitar signed by Sting" among other high-end music items. The ad for the Bose Music intelligent playback system highlights "its unique ability to listen to the music you play and learn our preferences based on your likes, dislikes, or even your mood at the moment." There are numerous ads for satellite radio systems and the luxury SUVs that include them as standard equipment.

Such marketing sometimes resonates with the adults it targets. George is a 51-year-old, Anglo electrical engineer who just installed a satellite radio system in his Lexus sedan. He sees two benefits of his musical purchase: "I don't have to mess with CDs or radio anymore. I get to play only the music I like to hear . . . There are stations dedicated just to '80s heavy metal. Cool." George has effectively eliminated the hassles of concert crowds and debates over musical tastes with peers. High technology puts his e-self in control of his musical environment. George can experience his music with the aura of cultural independence affluent adults seek.

The Self as Lover

A significant aspect of the continuous popularity of rock 'n' roll music is its use in helping make sense of others, especially in intimate relationships. Numerous observers have correctly identified the sexist messages present in rock (e.g., McRobbie 1978). A postmodern existentialist view, however, highlights the fact that rock 'n' roll music displays an open-ended horizon of meaning for its audiences. What a rock 'n' roll music performance means is largely a function of the situation in which it is experienced and the particular self-needs of the audience member (Kotarba 1994a). As time passes, the rock 'n' roll audience matures, biographies evolve, men's and women's relationships change, popular music commodities come and go, cultural themes available through the media advance, and we would expect the actual lived experience of popular music to change.

A particular self-need of the mature rock 'n' roll fan is to interpret *romantic* phenomena. This can happen two ways. First, fans can (re)interpret music to fit romantic needs. In Joe's autobiographical writing as a rock 'n' roll fan (Kotarba 1997), he described the way he used Dion's 1961 classic song "Runaround Sue" to account for the way a girl back in eighth grade rejected his very timid show of affection in favor of that of a more aggressive, older teenaged boy. Like the Sue in the song, Joe's Sue was a *bad* girl and he was merely a victim of her wiles. Twenty-five years later, at a class reunion, he used the same song as the basis for a conversation with the same Sue. They laughed about the silliness of those elementary school days, but Joe's heartbeat jumped a bit when she admitted that she really did like him back then but was too shy to tell him!

Second, fans can gravitate towards music that can be perceived as romantic. Autobiographically speaking (Joe), "Smokey" Robinson and the Miracles' "Tracks of My Tears" was a constant play on my 45 rpm record player in 1965 when it put comforting words to yet another heartbreak in my life. I would not have been drawn as much to this new record if I did not have a personal need for its plaintive prose. In general, fans gravitate towards music that fits their everyday life concerns.

Baby boomers use rock 'n' roll materials for a range of romantic purposes. They use music (e.g., CDs and DVDs) as birthday and Christmas gifts. They use music to help them appreciate other media such as films and television. One of the more interesting romantic uses of rock 'n' roll music is the *our-song* phenomenon, in which a musical performance serves to define a relationship. Our-songs are clearly not limited to baby boomers. Pre-adolescents, for example, commonly choose songs that remind them of a boy or a girl, but are often too shy to disclose this fact to the other, as we have seen!

For mature rock 'n' roll fans, the our-song can function at least two ways. First, it provides meaning for benchmark events in the relationship. Shirley is a 52-year-old, Latina sales person who is a big Los Lobos fan. She builds anniversary activities around one particular song she and her husband both enjoy:

> We fell in love with "Nadie Quiere Sufrir" at a Los Lobos concert when we were still just dating. It is a very pretty waltz that actually comes from an Edith Piaf song . . . I make sure the CD (with the song) is in the car when we drive to (our anniversary) dinner. He bought me the CD for our anniversary a few years ago . . . Oh, I guess it just makes us feel young again.

Second, the our-song can help the person feel like a lover. As couples age and perhaps find themselves feeling and acting less romantic over time, the our-song can function as a quick emotional fix. Rob is a 58-year-old, Anglo executive who has maintained a serious relationship with Tommy, a 47-year-old artist, for about fifteen years. Their song is Queen's "Bohemian Rhapsody:"

> There will never be another Freddie Mercury. It was really special to have our own gay rock icon . . . I surprise Tommy by playing "Bohemian Rhapsody" now and again. Tommy is still thrilled that I remember it . . . Why? Well, it's one of those songs that make you feel good, to feel that you can be gay and a rocker at the same time . . . I like doing things for Tommy. We are just so busy with our careers, 'makes us feel like an old married couple!

Needless to say, the popular music industry is aware of the market for rock 'n' roll goods and services. One of the more recent examples is the advent and growing popularity of rock 'n' roll cruises. Carnival Cruise Lines offers the following "rock 'n' roll Cruise Vacation" in an on-line ad:

> What could be cooler than a seven-day Caribbean cruise with legendary big-hair 1970s/80s rockers Journey, Styx and REO Speedwagon? Well . . . we'll reserve comment. But, if your idea of a totally awesome vacation is a seven-day cruise with legendary big-hair 1970s/80s rockers Journey, Styx and REO Speedwagon, you're in luck.

Interactionist sociologists—as you can glean from the above—are not only interested in what individuals experience throughout life course, but also in "how the life course is interpretively constructed and used by persons to make sense of experience" (Holstein and Gubrium 2003: 841). In order to construct meaning, Holstein and Gubrium tell us, we utilize *narrative resources:* tools for building, shaping and re-shaping, and making sense of the becoming of self. Music is a narrative resource. By employing narrative resources and constructing a sense of self endowed with a feeling of continuity and growth we engage in *biographical work* (ibid.).

The Self as Parent and Grandparent

As we have shown in Chapter 1, the impact of rock 'n' roll on one's self as parent is possibly the most pervasive aspect of the personal rock 'n' roll biography. Baby boomers grew up experiencing music as a major medium for communicating with parents. Managing music illustrates one's skill at parenting, as well as one's style of parenting.

There is a greater tendency among parents—apparently across ethnic groups and social classes—to manage rock 'n' roll as though their teen-agers are children who need to be nurtured and protected rather than as adolescents who must be controlled, sanctioned, and feared. Mass media-generated images of obstinate if not rebellious youth generally ignore the reflexive relationship between teenagers and their parents. Parents then respond to the identities they helped create by controlling, criticizing, sanctioning, and punishing their teenagers for living out their rock 'n' roll-inspired identities—responding to them as if they were autonomous, responsible adults.

This *congenial* style of being a parent appears to extend into the next cycle of life: that of grandparent. As Mogelonsky (1996) and other family researchers have noted, grandparents have a tendency to interact with their grandchildren in ways very similar to the ways they interacted with their own children. If pop music was an important feature to them as parents, it will be the same as grandparents. What changes, of course, are styles of music, music technology and the moral context of pop music. Frank is a 61-year-old retired public school teacher who has two grandchildren: 17-year-old Bobby and 11-year-old Denise. Bobby has been easy to please with musical gifts and experiences. Just as he did with his own son thirty years ago or so, Frank has given Bobby birthday and Christmas gifts of music, but according to current styles: iTune gift cards, an iPod mini, and tickets to a Radiohead concert. However, Frank will not share musical experiences with Bobby because:

"Bobby listens to a lot of rap, and I just cannot stand that stuff." Denise presented other kinds of difficulties. In addition to a Carrie Underwood CD she wanted for Christmas, she begged Frank for tickets to see Hannah Montana in concert at Reliant Stadium in Houston. Her father told her that the family could not afford tickets, so she strategically asked her doting grandpa. Frank's response was "how can I tell my little girl no?," but the task of actually getting tickets was monumental:

> I heard that all tickets sold out in about ten minutes. I went on-line and couldn't get in for almost a half-hour. I actually drove down to the Reliant box office later that morning, and it was the same story. I then went on-line to eBay and paid $400 for two

(nose) bleeds . . . You're old enough to remember when concert tickets were ten bucks at the door. Man, how things have changed, but I promised her.

The Self as Believer

As we have seen, baby boomers' early experiences of rock 'n' roll music were complex. They learned to love, play, dissent, and through the idiom. They also experienced spirituality (Seay and Neely 1986). In adulthood, the spiritual dimension of rock 'n' roll continues to impact the self as believer. The lyrics and mood created by such performers as Van Morrison (*Astral Weeks*) and U2 (*The Joshua Tree*) provide baby boomers with non-sectarian yet religion-friendly soundtracks. New Age music, such as that produced by Windham Hill, functions the same way.

Rock and pop music have also had a direct influence on spirituality by helping shape organized religious ceremonies and rituals to fit the tastes of the adult members. For example, Catholic baby boomers grew up at a time when the Church, largely as a result of the Vatican II Council, encouraged parishes to make use of local musical styles and talent. Witness the emergence of the rock 'n' roll mass in the 1970s. Today, the very popular style of praise and worship music, with its electronic keyboard and modern melodies, is infiltrating Catholic liturgy.

An integral segment of the self-as-parent is moral if not religious or spiritual socialization. Rock and pop function as mechanisms for teaching religious beliefs and values in many families, whether or not rock is compatible with the particular family's religious orientation. For mainstream Protestant denominations, rock 'n' roll increasingly fits with the faith. Take, for example, the success of Jars of Clay—a soft rock Christian band—or Creed, an edgier and equally spiritual ensemble. In these cases too, we can see how music functions as a resource selected by fans and made meaningful in their building of a sense of identity.

The Self as Political Actor

Rock 'n' roll music serves as a soundtrack for the situations in which baby boomers perceive themselves as political actors. rock 'n' roll can add both atmosphere and meaning to political events. For example, New York punk poet and singer Patti Smith performed a concert in Houston on March 28, 2003—right at the beginning of the war in Iraq. The concert was originally scheduled simply to support an exhibit of her art displayed at the Museum of Contemporary Arts. The audience was overwhelmingly middle-aged people, dressed up in their jeans and long (hippie) skirts. Through conversations with numerous fans after the concert, it was clear that they *enjoyed* the concert. Patti Smith's poetry and songs (e.g., "People Have the Power") gave them a relevant and identifiable venue for sharing their overwhelmingly negative *feelings* about the war.

Families also use rock and pop to relay a sense of political history to their children. For example, every year on Memorial Day in Houston, various veterans' organizations sponsor a concert and rally at the Miller Outdoor Theater. Most of the veterans present fought in the Vietnam and Gulf Wars, two wars for which rock 'n' roll served as the musical soundtrack. Most of the veterans bring their children to the event. Among all the messages and information available to the kids is the type of music popular during the war. A popular band regularly invited to perform is the Canadian band Guess Who, whose "American Woman" was a major anthem among soldiers. Joe has observed fathers explaining the song to their teenaged and preteen children, who would otherwise view it as just another of dad's old songs. The fathers explain that the song had different meanings for different men. For some, it reminded them of girlfriends back home who broke up with them during the war. For others, the title was enough to remind them of their faithful girlfriends back home. For still others, the song reminded them of the occasions when they were sitting around camp, smoking pot and listening to any North American rock 'n' roll songs available as a way of bridging the many miles between them and home. In Houston, Juneteenth and Cinco de Mayo activities function much the same way for African-American and Hispanic families, respectively. In summary, rock 'n' roll music is vital to maintaining a sense of the political self because many baby boomers learned their politics—and how to be and feel political—from Country Joe McDonald (and the Fish), Jimi Hendrix, and the Grateful Dead.

CONCLUSION

We have described several contemporary experiences and manifest-ations of self to illustrate the ways the rock idiom has remained a major cultural force in the life course of mature fans. There are obviously other experiences. Furthermore, these experiences are not limited to fans. Rock music is also a preeminent aspect of the musician's self who performed rock music many years ago, and who continues to perform. These musicians redirect their careers in directions more comfortable if not more profitable. Kinky Friedman comes to mind. He was a Texas-based band leader in the 1970s (The infamous Texas Jew Boys). He now performs acoustically in small clubs, while managing a very successful line of men's clothing and authoring popular mystery novels. As time passes (Kotarba 2002b), rock 'n' roll provides narrative resources for the aging self's biographical work. In interviews Joe routinely hears respondents note how the recent deaths of middle-aged rock 'n' roll artists, such as Robert Palmer and George Harrison, are disturbing because these afflictions may be more the result of aging than the excessive lifestyles associated with the premature deaths of artists such as Janice Joplin, Jimmy Hendrix, and Jim Morrison. It will be interesting, then, to see the various ways in which baby boomers draw upon the rock idiom as they move beyond middle age. For example, what new meanings will aging boomers attach to the rock idiom? What place will rock have in the grandparent–grandchild relationship? Attending to such questions will highlight the role that music plays in the ongoing becoming-of-self.

7

GLOBALIZATION

The sociological study of globalization can take many forms. Sociologists study economic and political world systems, the emergence of a global risk society, dynamics of colonization and cultural imperialism, and the growing environmental interconnectedness of the globe, to mention only a few of the approaches to the general topic. In keeping with our attention to the mundane experience of culture and popular music, in this chapter we focus on issues of cultural globalization and its experience in everyday life. Before we proceed to defining what we mean by both globalization and by cultural globalization, let us introduce an example which will serve to illustrate our focus and perspective. Phillip tells this story.

In the summer of 2001 I was enjoying a few weeks' vacation in the Nepali Himalayas, away from the stresses of graduate school and from the modern comforts of the western world. One day, in the sweltering heat (for us Canadians, at least) and noise of Kathmandu, my girlfriend and I decided to abandon the city and satisfy our thirst for authentic travel by embarking on a three-week trek through the Annapurna Mountain range. The Annapurna range sits across the Northern side of Nepal, bordering Tibet, and not too far from the more famous trekking area surrounding Mt. Everest. Compared to the latter, we felt that Annapurna was a much more off-the-beaten track trek (pardon the pun) and one that promised to give us a more authentic look into the lives of rural and mountainous peoples of the Himalayas. So, off we went. The journey by a series of local buses took us through narrow-winding roads, remote villages, and landslide-swept grounds that our bus driver gingerly (at least so he must have thought) negotiated. When after ten hours we reached the physical end of the unpaved road we unloaded, tightened up our climbing boots' laces, saddled ourselves with our backpacks, and ventured off on the mountain trail with our local Nepali guide, Uttar. As we waded through small creeks, dodged trail-hogging water buffalos, negotiated blood-sucking leeches hiding in the thick vegetation around the trail, and braved the unpredictability of the mixed alpine-tropical climate, we sought occasional refuge in small tea houses: guest houses open for both travelers and the numerous local porters transporting goods of all kinds on their own backs and shoulders up the steep, rocky, narrow mountainous trail. Figure 7.1 shows the "downtown core" of one village—visually, one like many villages—that we cruised through.

Figure 7.1 Despite the remoteness of the village and its inaccessibility by anything other than by foot (or donkey), locals happily provide information in English and cater to travelers' need for conveniences, such as ice cold drinks and American-style apple pie (Photo: Phillip Vannini)

We took the picture shown in Figure 7.1 from a tea house at which we stayed overnight. From the angle at which it was taken it is impossible to see the much of the inside of the tea house itself, so the reader's imagination is needed to complete the image. If you have never traveled through this neck of the woods imagine a physical context in which most of the modern conveniences generally found in accommodations are absent. The bathroom of our guest house was an outhouse, latrine-style. No telephones, no television sets, no radios were available in our room or in the house. Running water was also unavailable. Electricity worked on and off, but mostly off, especially when needed on. In short, it was paradise for us adventure-seekers.

As I snapped the picture, I quickly dropped my backpack and sat down, sprawling my legs across another chair, and let out a loud groan. It had been a long and exhausting day of trekking. As Uttar scooted into the kitchen to find either the hosts or some ready-made tea left behind for us by them, April—my girlfriend—hollered at me from the other side of the porch and with a tone of urgency asked for our camera.

"I just put it away in the backpack"—I replied—"there's no way I'm getting up again."

"Then just turn around for now, and look what's behind your back"—she said—"I know you'll want to take a picture later."

Curious, I turned around to face the wall. Figure 7.2 is the picture she wanted me to take.

Music is everywhere (and quite possibly Guns 'n Roses too). Arguably the most effective global medium of communication, music is a universal language that people can immediately relate to and share. Music, as a form of culture, travels. On its travels it transits through and stops in places far away from its origin changing lives and in turn itself. This is, in a way, what we mean by cultural globalization: we mean a process whereby cultural symbols and objects move away, with consequential outcomes, from the contexts in which they originate regardless (and sometimes in spite) of geographic and political boundaries and distance. Throughout this process of movement both cultural expressions and human members of cultures become something new, different. With globalization, a new world emerges. A Nepali farmer may become a butt-rock fan after listening to a forgotten mixed tape featuring songs from Guns 'n Roses. An American draft-dodger expatriate may get back in touch with his hippie youth by listening to Tibetan chants while taking a Yoga class in his new hometown in Western Canada. A Polish teenager may use the rebel yell of American rock 'n' roll to resist both Catholic and the Communist ideologies. And a Houstonian may wear his *Latino* and rock fan identity,

Figure 7.2 This Guns 'n Roses poster dated back to the 1980s (Photo: Phillip Vannini)

simultaneously, with a badge of pride. In sum, globalization refers to a dynamic inherent to any form of culture: movement. By examining the movement of music away from "original" contexts and into "new" contexts and traditions, in this chapter we reflect on issues of hybridity and authenticity, on the nature of the global and the local, and on the "global generalized other" in relation to whom many musical, and non-musical, identities are shaped. We begin with an overview of the idea of cultural globalization. As an aid for our discussion we focus on the genre of world music and its authenticity. We then present two case studies. The first case study examines the evolution of popular music in the central European country of Poland, especially since the demise of communism in 1989. The major theme we will discuss is the way the major political and economic changes taking place in Poland over the past twenty years have been accompanied by the concurrent Westernization and fragmentation of the popular music experience in Poland. This musical experience, consequently, is contributing to Polish youth's ability and desire to shape their culture increasingly like "teenagers" in the West have for the past sixty years. The second case study examines the development of *rock en Español* in the United States. This style of music reflects the distinctive musical and cultural needs and tastes of its upwardly mobile, largely Mexican-American, audiences.

MUSIC, CULTURE, AND GLOBALIZATION

If there was one reason why seeing that Guns 'n Roses poster upset me so much—beside the fact that I've never liked Axl and his buddies—it's because I felt that its presence corrupted the cultural authenticity of the idyllic Himalayan mountain setting. Seeing traces of Western "civilization" is not what I had bargained for. I wanted to see a society suspended somewhere between the Middle Ages and the turn of the twentieth century; I wanted pure foreignness in its exotic allure; I wanted Tibetan chants and the echo of prayer bells, not images of hair metal. I wanted, in other words, to be in contact with the "Other" in its authentic, genuine, unmediated, unadulterated identity. Yet, this was pure selfishness on my part. That identity is one that *I* had given this "Other." That authenticity is a myth, as I realized: a fruit of my Western imagination and my romantic attitude. The world is forever changing, and to believe in the authenticity of the "original" is to forget that the original is too a product of that constant change and of imagination in the first place.

My girlfriend and I learned our lesson gradually throughout our trip. Our hope to find a piece of authenticity continually faded farther and farther away. For example, we once thought of buying CDs of traditional Tibetan music only to feel that the very *recording* and *selling* of those performances—no matter how ethnographically "real"—on *foreign technologies,* for *foreign audiences* made the whole thing feel very inauthentic. Not to mention that we were seeking *Tibetan* music in *Nepal . . .*! Seeking authenticity gave way to the realization that all we could find was a *hybrid* instead. Why was this? Because the West and the North have colonized the East and the South? Because the world is resembling more and more the one part of it that has achieved global economic dominance? And in doing so, has the West choked the rest of the world, turned it into its periphery, and annihilated cultural unique-ness in the name of a commodified sameness? Maybe; yet this seems like a partial account at best. Let us reflect.

There are various accounts of globalization. A facile definition of this phenomenon views it as the commodification and colonization of the globe by the hand of transnational corporations and their inter-national governmental supporters and alliances like NAFTA, GATT, etc. According to this view, the West, and for the most part North America and Europe, but increasingly also Japan and Australia, is the perpetrator of a crime of cultural genocide. This is not a bloody crime, but a subtle one based on the endless seduction of Coca-Cola bottles, Big Macs, shiny new cars, and Guns 'n Roses too, all put together and wrapped in Christmas gift paper. Proponents of this perspective view globalization as another instance of cultural and economic imperialism: a symbolic and material colonization that works unidirectionally from the stronger to the weaker, destroying everything in its path.

Someone resisting these colonizing forces is not unlikely to idealize a mythical past and a distant place where local culture was still uncorrupted from outside contact. As one of those romantic people, in my own naïveté I used to believe that the mentioned corner of Nepal would be safe from the power of Western culture. I idealized a "pure" "Other," and when I saw that in its actuality it did not correspond to my vision of authenticity I became upset over the fact that the West had colonized it. But in doing so I violated that "Other" twice: first in shaping an image of it based on *my* desire of how it should it be, and, second, in victimizing it, that is, in believing it to be weak and powerless to a foreign culture's expansionist energy. My resistance was misplaced.

In an attempt to portray a less simplistic understanding of globalization, some scholars have argued that globalization is not synonymous with uniformity, but instead with creolization (Hannerz 1987), indigenization (Robertson 1992), and hybridization (Canclini 1995). All of these root images point not to a unidirectional movement of cultural standardization, but to a complex network of influences that criss-cross the globe and turn it into a heightened version of what it has always been: a large and diverse, but deeply interconnected and forever changing place. This understanding of globalization hinges on the idea that continuous exchanges between economic cores and peripheries end up mixing the traditional (e.g. the pre-modern) and the modern, the Western and the Eastern, thus confusing facile representations of who is the dominant force, and who is the dominated one. In this sense the hybrid blurs distinctions between the local and the distant: what is *here* is not necessarily diametrically opposed to what is *there*, and therefore what is there is not exempt from influences of whatever comes from here.

British sociologist Anthony Giddens has advanced one of the clearest conceptualizations of globalization. While admitting that the world has always been interconnected Giddens (2000) demonstrates that increases in the speed at which international economic, political, technological, and cultural transactions take place have decentered the world—that is, taken power away from its "core"—and resulted in the diffusion of diversity, the emphasis on the uniqueness (albeit hybrid) of local cultures and identities. In other words, while the world has witnessed examples of deterritorialization (loss of original sense of place, as it were) during the colonial and imperial era of the early and middle twentieth century, it is now witnessing the phenomenon of reterritorialization: old places are being recreated anew. For example, Guns 'n Roses fans are showing up among the Nepalese. Another example ought to be developed and elaborated upon at this point. To stress the significance of a multi-directional and multi-dimensional view of globalization, let us examine the movement of musical cultures from the East to the West.

World Music Flows

I (again, Phillip) live on Vancouver Island, on the West Coast of British Columbia, Canada. Vancouver Island is surrounded by an archipelago of small islands (with populations ranging from 30 to 15,000) up and down its eastern side. By way of ethnographic investigation I have been studying the everyday life rituals and culture of these islands for quite some time now. One of the characteristics of these islands' culture is that of a hypersensitivity to the importance of movement. Many islanders, it seems, are constantly on the move; either because they need to catch the ferry to go to school, work, or to the supermarket, or doctor's office, or because they need to, or wish to, travel across the globe. The ferries that connect these islands—as the only mode of transportation on and off—are very interesting portals of their movement. The excerpt from my field notes below tells of a unique cultural expression, and more precisely an element of a unique musical scene, moving through one of these ferries, when a world music performer came to the islands:

August 2007: I have been wondering for some time now what this guy looked like in person. His picture—posted on any key bulletin board around, from the ferry's to the grocery stores'—is one of a kind: smacking of a hybrid-like aura like nothing I've seen before. The Sandokan-style moustache and beard, the Jesus hairstyle, the loose Indian-style satin dress, the Yoga leg-crossover, the made-in-Kathmandu incense burning in the background that I could almost smell just by looking at the photo. And yet he looks like any ole yippie from West Vancouver who traded in his blue chip stocks for a lot of flights to Thailand and Bangalore. A few days ago, on a different trip, I wrote down somewhere in my notes an insight into what he does: he does the world. Under the aegis of aural meditation, sonorous relaxation, and soundscape-production what he does is no different from what any minor rock band on a world tour does: he is a small-scale global merchant of culture. He's on the ferry today. Even he has to take the ferry to come over to the island. I'd better go over and talk to him. I'm curious to see what he's all about.

"How's it going, man?"—I open up.

"Beautiful sky, isn't it?"—he replies.

"I heard about your upcoming performance. Sorry I won't be able to make it on that day."

"Are you into the many musical styles of the world?"

"Only when they are into me."

We both laugh at my stupid joke. We begin to talk. He is a world music connoisseur, though he wouldn't say it like that. He's a healer, a mystic, and a student of the enchanting powers of poly-harmonic music. He put it like that. His "show"—forgive the shorthand—is about involving his audience into a collective state of higher awareness of the senses of olfaction and hearing, as well as the sixth and seventh senses. By awakening people through his own fusion music, and his favourite world music tunes as well, he leads them into transporting their selves out of their bodies into a collective state of ecstatic, harmonious being. He's on a "tour" of the Gulf Islands of the Strait of Georgia. Not too far from where he tells ms he was born: North Vancouver. I was close.

"A lot of people come to these shows?"—I inquire.

"Given the low number of souls who live on these small islands, yes. In relative terms this area is incredibly into different musical styles and diverse spiritual experiences."

I know the answer to the next question, but I want to hear it from him: "Why is that?"

"Well, a lot of people who live around here are global nomads. Many are draft dodgers from the U.S., from the hippie era, you know? A lot of them are continental Europeans who left the old continent in search of a closer connection with land and waterscape. Some are older Canadians who want to slow down their life's pace. And just about all of them are global travellers by lifestyle, very in tune with the possibility that their lifestyle is not the only lifestyle in the world, you know?"

Do I ever. I live around here. And I fit box category number two and four in his list. So, what's a nice African drum-beat doing in a cold and rainy place like this, one might wonder? What is the truthfulness of a Hindu-style aural meditation experience when it's rigidly scheduled for a 5.30 to 6.45 pm slot at the community center, right after the kids' kayak lesson and right before the only Sushi takeout place on the island closes for the night? And what is the authenticity of a soundscape that fuses the rhythms of cultures as separate as Sufi, Tuva, Tibet, and

Sumatra? Those are good questions. Yet, the most obvious answer, one that points to the phoniness of all of this, would entirely miss the point.

The global movement of music has certainly become more rapid and widespread with the advent of modern ways of travel and communication. It is now possible for anyone with the economic means to engage in a little globalizing act of their own. You can try this at home: travel to a distant country, take over there signs of your culture, and bring back home signs of their own culture. In a way, that is what my newly made acquaintance is doing by bringing traces of world musical forms over the ferry. Globalization does not happen somewhere in the abstract, over our heads. It happens through a multitude of individual and collective acts: from migration and diasporas (the displacement of entire peoples), to marketing and exchange. As metropolitan centers connect to remote peripheries, some musical forms and expressions travel with the people and communication media that carry them. In doing so, music momentarily misses the connection with its geographic origin, yet without abandoning its roots forever. In other words, movement is not the precondition of inauthenticity, as some might argue. Let us explain.

Imagine a group of people rooted in the social and cultural traditions of a distinct place. Imagine them getting together one day to express themselves freely through music. Unscripted, unrecorded, uninterested in selling their music to others they create and perform genuine music right there and then. There you have it: ground zero of cultural authenticity, right? As any one might argue, *any* follow-up of that act is a step away from the authenticity of that ground zero expression. Their argument—let's call it the ground-zero view of authenticity—is simple and captivating: authenticity decreases the farther away we move from ground zero: spatially, temporally, socially (in terms of different performers and audiences), and sonorously (any encore is but an imitation, isn't it?). Indeed, this argument for the inauthenticity of second (or third, or fourth, etc.) degree performances has a lot of reasons to be built on: from the lack of understanding that second-degree audiences and performers may have for the first degree authentic act, to the in-authenticating condition of rootlessness of any second degree performance. Second-degree performances— that is, those performances which take place after the original per-formance—are but one or more steps away removed from the ground zero of authenticity, and often moved not by the willingness to express oneself but by things like greed, envy, lack of originality and creativity, the will to co-opt, bastardize, and appropriate for whatever reason.

Indeed, this removal of performance from its ground zero is the very reason why all of "world music" as a genre is deeply inauthentic—this ground-zero argument might go. "World music"—the category of music assembling sounds from all four corners of the globe (often in compilation CDs that feature nameless artists and tracks titled only after cliché descriptions or the effect they intend to evoke in the listener) that is found in a special section of your favorite music store—is but an invention. It shelves together musical expressions alien to one another and alien to their audiences, simply for the purpose of seducing potential buyers into a safe aural exploration of the globe. Sort of like a musical zoo which one visits much as you would visit an animal zoo: by experiencing decontextualized realities with no relation to one another or to the place where they have been forcefully assembled.

This ground-zero view of authenticity also has some historical evidence on its side. The expression "world music" dates back to 1987 when record company executives met in London to examine ways of marketing popular music from many part of the world to British audiences. World music became a catch-all expression, a marketing ploy imitated in German-speaking markets (*weltbeat*) and French ones as well (*musique mondiale*). In 1991, Billboard devised a chart of its own for world music, and a Grammy category was formed. From thereon the commercialization of world music can be seen as a textbook exercise in the social construction of meaning. As Pacini-Hernandez (1993: 50) has noted, world music is

> a marketing term describing the products of musical cross-fertilisation between the north—the U.S. and Western Europe—and south—primarily Africa and the Caribbean basin ... established specifically to cultivate and nurture the appetites of First World listeners for exotic new sounds from the Third World.

Similarly critical is Erlmann (1996: 474) who notes that the term world music "displays a peculiar, self-congratulatory pathos: a mesmerising formula for a new business venture, a kind of shorthand figure for a new—albeit fragmented—global economic reality with alluring commercial prospects." Those who argue for the inauthenticity of world music point to the forceful appropriation enacted by the West. Consuming distant musical styles—this argument goes—demands that distal musical performers and performances be packaged as pre-modern, natural, exotic, and raw. The forced convergence of these sounds not only results in their commodification, but also in their displacement, fetishization, and marginalization. It is no accident that the marketing of world music involves also the marketing of New

Age practices that promise new experiences for Western bodies: from transcendence to meditation, from somatic exploration to unchoreo-graphed dance and movement, together with the self-help books and merchandise that accompany these adventures in alternative shop-ping. Indeed—as the critical argument insightfully goes—the world of African souls and Asian healers is one closer to the bodily, animal element, and more distant from the typically white and European rational mind and thus appealing to the fetishizing gaze of the latter (Gilroy 1993).

While it is difficult, if not impossible to disagree with this ground-zero view of the inauthenticity of world music, the wholesale of a cultural performance as inauthentic is nothing but a partial argument if we fail to understand it as a phenomenon that is based not only on production and distribution, but also on consumption. Arguments based on a bottom-up perspective to cultural production are necessar-ily limited in the twofold sense that just as any attempt of any corporate marketer to package a musical product with meaning is limited by the interpretive power of its consumers, any attempt of any academic or critic to deem something inauthentic is counterbalanced by the possibility that an audience might consume that product authentically.

Consider the reception of world music in the geographical and social context of the islands I mentioned at the beginning of this section. As my "world music merchant" informant insightfully stated, the reception of a musical expression that has traveled far away from where it originated is a peculiar one among audiences who also have traveled far from where they originated. Just as people move across societies and cultures without reducing the possibility they might experience a sense of authenticity in their life, cultural expressions can cross geographical and social boundaries without necessarily corrupting their authen-ticity. A globalized world is one in which locality can no longer be understood as confined within a tightly bound place and time. A restriction of authenticity to such a small-scale idea of locality would result in paradoxical outcomes: any cultural expression would have to be restricted to its ground zero lest it become corrupt. In other words, throw out of the window your Youssou N'Dour and Ravi Shankar recordings. With this definition of authenticity they are now phony by definition, and you are a sucker if you enjoy them.

Or, perhaps, chuck the ground-zero view of authenticity out of the window and replace it with a notion of authenticity that makes space for the hybrid. What a concept of authenticity based on hybridity—rather than one which juxtaposes hybridity and authenticity as binary oppositions—can do, is increase the potential for cross-fertilization, fusion, original pastiche, and experimentation (if you're looking for a good musical example of this, check out Youssou N'Dour and Neneh Cherry's "7 seconds" song and video). A ground-zero view of authenticity freezes authenticity in the past and confines it to a narrow and inaccessible (at least for most unlucky ones) place. According to the ground-zero view of authenticity, the only performance, performers, and audiences that count as authentic are the first. Academics and critics thus function as gatekeepers, reminding all those who attempt to reproduce the first degree performance that they are but doomed to be inauthentic. Such attempts, therefore, are but colonizing, co-opting, and imperializing acts. This is a view of authenticity that perhaps had some validity in a distant, modern world but one that is becoming increasingly utopian, elitist, and unmindful of the greater mobility, speed of change, and degree of transience of an interconnected globe and peoples interested more in exploration, inspiration, and innovation than conservation of tradition.

So, let us go back to the production, distribution, and consumption of that fusion-driven soundscape ready for the aural meditation of island-dwelling Western Canadians. Is that a trick being played on them, or is it an opportunity for them to connect authentically with a new musical experience? As a few of these islanders tell me, the opportunity to live their life in the place and community of their choice, engaging in the lifestyle they prefer to practice, is a deeply authenticating one. Music, as well as other visual and performance arts, plays an important role in their life and their communities. And so does respect for other cultures and the environment in which they live. These are people who are aware of the hybrid character of their small island societies. For many of them connecting to the sounds of Nepali folk song brings them back to the times when in their young adulthood they danced as hippies on Freak Street in downtown Kathmandu. For others meditation and relaxation with the sounds of the island of Sumatra is a natural choice when the relaxing sounds and sights of their own small island life surround them daily. For others understanding the melancholic melodies of diasporic sounds comes easy when they too are the sons and daughters of diaspora and expatriation. In sum, the possibility that a musical expression may be authentically experienced is there even when this is far removed from its ground zero.

Musical hybridity is not opposed to authenticity. The movement of migrants, refugees, expatriates, nomads, and diasporic people—and the consequent movement of their cultural rituals and expressions alongside with them—as well as the increased flows of culture due to the more advanced communication technologies now available have contributed to changing the meanings of time and space, and thus to the formation of a heterophonic global musical scene in which pastiche, irony, and contradictions are the norm rather than the exception. Music, thanks to the potential for fluid cross-cultural communication its sonorous qualities offer, opens up spaces where authentic experiences may occur even when its production and distribution dynamics are enacted in spite of that possibility. Authenticity and hybridity are not opposed to one another, but entangled in configurations only typical of an interconnected world. As Frith (2000) has suggested, hybridity may very well be "the new authenticity."

Visions of authenticity based in a ground-zero ideology oppose much too simplistically authenticity and inauthenticity, make authentic cultural and musical expression something that no one can enjoy, and something based on isolation of musical communities rather than dialog amongst them. Furthermore, loading authenticity with meanings derived from ideologies of resistance politicizes music at the expense of what it is intended to be. And third, it equates the movement of culture with unidirectional colonization. Such view is contrary to the evidence of globalization. Such a world—and the idea of authenticity that best fits it—can only be understood through sociological lenses that investigate complex realities from the perspective of those who live them, rather than from the pulpits of those utopian critics who wish things would be otherwise. As Frith (1991: 267) has put it, this requires that older visions of authenticity and "the cultural imperialism model of nation versus nation must be replaced with a postimperial model of an infinite number of local experiences of (and responses to) something globally shared."

POPULAR MUSIC AND THE EMERGENCE OF THE "TEENAGER" IN POLAND

The changes taking place in Central and Eastern European societies in the late 1980s through the present have been broad and complex. Beginning with Poland, the former satellites and client states of the Soviet Union have all experienced various degrees of democratization, capitalization, and Westernization. Many people living in Central and Eastern Europe have worked feverishly to catch up with the West, largely in economic, cultural and political terms. The contemporary culture of the West which they covet, and which Frederick Jameson (1991) and many other observers have referred to as postmodernism, is most notably marked by a shift in the economy from production to consumption, the disappearance of the distinction between high and popular art, and the near hegemony of the mass media and the popular culture they distribute. Teenagers are at the forefront of this frenzied cultural activity.

Harvey (1989) argues that the two defining characteristics of postmodern culture in the late capitalistic West are ephemerality and fragmentation. Elements and styles of our way of life are increasingly both fleeting and diffuse. Harvey's discussion of the net consequence of postmodern culture on personality, motivation, and behavior on an individualistic level is of direct relevance to the present discussion. A powerful metaphor for individual experience is schizophrenia. In its common, as opposed to clinical, sense, the individual is schizophrenic to the degree he or she is neither capable of nor desirous of integrating the past, present, and future. Cultural items are subject to rapid transformation, and perspectives on time are overwhelmingly reduced to the present. By applying Harvey's argument to the status of "teenager" in late capitalistic society, we expect to find a young person who organizes personal identity around ever-changing styles, a very situational and selective use of history, and an overwhelming dependence on mass mediated resources for identity construction. In this section, we will describe ethnographically—that is, based upon direct observation and occasional personal experience—the relationship of the rapid and recent movement towards late capitalism and postmodernism in Poland to the self-identity of the Polish teenager. We will present vignettes from various conversations Joe has had with Polish teenagers regarding their everyday lives and musical experiences since democratization. Joe conducted his study while visiting Poland in 1992 and 2000 (Kotarba 2002c and 2008).

A Brief History of Popular Music and Youth in Poland Before 1989

The history of popular music in Poland is notably marked by a long and rich love affair between young people and rock 'n' roll music (Kan and Hayes 1994). Ryback (1990) and other observers have cited 1957 as the year several Polish bands began playing their versions of "Rock Around the Clock" and "Don't Be Cruel." Since then, the Polish rock scene has produced numerous artists performing music ranging from punk and heavy metal to pop rock and rap. Rock music is very popular among Polish youth. Sasinska-Klas (1993) found in her survey, for example, that over 90 percent of Polish youth aged 16–25 preferred Western-style rock to any other musical genre.

As George Lipsitz (1994: 138) notes, popular music specifically plays a complicated yet critical role in times of great political fervent, for "It helps to construct the nation state while at the same time being constructed by it." Accordingly, rock music has served as a political medium for youth during the cyclical episodes of economic and political unrest that marked Poland's history under communism. Pekacz (1992) assessed the quality and integrity of Polish rock music in terms of its status as an instrument of protest. In the 1970s, Polish rock music did not protest directly against the communist authorities, but, "instead, it was focused upon broad, 'existential' or 'all-human' universal issues in a post-hippie style" (Ibid.: 205). With the imposition of martial law in the 1980s, the government used rock music to co-opt potentially revolutionary feelings among youth. The emergence of punk rock in the 1980s did produce militant, anti-government music.

Kan and Hayes describe how the most popular punk band, Perfect, performed concerts for workers in Warsaw to celebrate the spread of Solidarity's strike from Gdansk to the rest of Poland. One song in particular, Perfect's 1981 hit "Autobiography," became the revolutionary anthem for angry Polish youth. The lyrics say:

> My father was working at a steel plant God knows where I also roughed up my hands I wore out my guitar and played millions of worthless tunes I learnt about sex There were three of us, each different Let's leave, the police are waiting for us, although others are busy stealing now But, well . . . This world is unbelievable our music causes fear our music causes fear.
>
> (translated to English by Kan and Hayes, 1994: 50–51)

The punk movement in Poland, as elsewhere, largely vanished by the mid-1980s. The most popular bands, including Perfect, turned to the search for commercial success. Huge crowds at rock music festivals—such as Jarocin which annually draws tens of thousands of fans—and large sales of cassettes largely replaced open political criticism. The Polish government supported rock music as an apolitical safety valve to channel young people's anger and energy, even to the point of providing radio programming for American heavy metal music (Weinstein 1991).

The everyday musical experiences of Polish youth before the revolution, especially those of the massive working class, directly reflected the drudgery of everyday life under communism. For example, O'Rourke (1988) visited Warsaw in 1986 and observed how the ultimate boredom produced by socialism led young people to drink themselves constantly into a stupor. For many, there was little prospect of a meaningful job, and even less prospect of a useful education. Alcohol and heavy metal music provided efficient analgesia from the pain of totalitarianism. Sadly, the ultimate economic poverty of socialism even precluded punk rockers from spiking and coloring their hair because of a shortage of commercially available cosmetics in Poland. Youth disappeared from public life by escaping into vodka and rock and roll.

Popular Music in Poland Since 1989

Since the revolution in 1989, the popular music scene in Poland has become increasingly fragmented. The move to a market economy has resulted in an explosion of the amount, quality and diversity of popular music available to young people. One of the dramatic examples of the rapid transition to a commodity economy was the explosion in the number of televisions, VCRs, cable television systems, and TV satellite dishes. The number of television stations in Wroclaw, for example, grew from two before the revolution to more than a dozen by 1992. The emergence of Western-style, mall-like music stores in all major cities brought compact disks into the marketplace. And, the widest range of music is now available to Polish kids through Internet services such as iTunes and Internet radio broadcasts. Major record companies like Sony and Warner Music are distributing CDs in Poland and developing local talent for eventual global marketing.

Consequently, the styles of popular music available to young people have expanded three ways. First, Polish youth now have access to all the popular music available to American or British youth. The traditional time lag between popularity in the States and popularity in secondary markets like Poland's has virtually disappeared. Polish youth no longer have to rely on Voice of America to broadcast popular American music, nor do they have to rely on poor quality bootleg tapes. Second, Polish artists are devising local versions of all this globalized music. For example, we now witness Polish rap music (Kazik), Polish "boy bands" (Just 5), and even Polish Celtic New Age Music (White Garden). Third, Polish artists have been creating much new music that is true to traditional musical styles. Cabaret music, performed in melancholy or torch style by a singer accompanied by piano or some other very simple instrumentation, has traditionally been very popular in Poland and remains so, for example, in the person of Anna Maria Jopek.

There are other indicators of the expansion of popular music in Poland. The market for "teen" music magazines, largely from Germany, exploded as local entrepreneurs began publishing Polish versions of them (e.g., *machina* and *Tylko Rock*). Western rock bands, such as the Rolling Stones and the Cure, began performing at concerts in Poland. Before the revolution, these concerts were very rare because the weak economy and the weak Polish Zloty resulted in widespread skepticism among rock performers that they would be paid for their concerts in currency with any kind of reasonable exchange value back in the West. There were also plans for Michael Jackson to finance the construction of an amusement/theme park near Warsaw, that have since been put on hold (*The Warsaw Voice* 1996).

Working-Class Teenagers: Life Beyond Heavy Metal

The working-class teens Joe talked with have experienced both the high expectations associated with democratization and, to a more modest degree, the early rewards of democratization. The important point is that their musical experiences have become very diverse.

The Center in Wroclaw is an after-school and weekend place for the teens to visit when they are not in school. These teens come from working-class families in rural areas in the Silesian or southwestern section of Poland. They are sent to Wroclaw to attend high school. They live either in dormitories or with host families. Since they live away from their own families, they are often lonely and emotionally "uneasy," as one young man put it. They use popular music as a source of comfort during times of loneliness. The boys at the Center prefer Western heavy metal music such as Queensryche and AC/DC. They relate to this music because it fits their concern for personal problems such as abusive families, conflict with teachers, problems with drugs, and so forth. Like their American counterparts, Polish "headbangers" commonly listened to speed metal music, such as Slayer and Metallica, as a way of relieving everyday life stress. The working-class girls at the Center preferred pop music, especially female performers such as Madonna and Beyonce. They not only appreciate songs about love and relationships, but they pay close attention to the fashion and style trends highlighted by these stars.

When Joe talked to these teens about their favorite songs, they generally indicated a preference for songs about relationships, parents, adults, morality and personal problems, regardless of the genre or style of rock music to which the kids were committed. The Polish rock song cited most frequently as the kids' favorite was "For Ann," by the group KULT, which they indicated is a song about boyfriends and girlfriends. Another favorite song was "Autobiography," by the group Perfect, which the kids said is about the complexity of growing up. One 16-year-old boy had been living in a high school dormitory for three months. He indicated that the song functions almost like a good friend for him: "I like the song because I have the same kinds of dreams. My life is like the song. . . . It warns against certain things in life. It helps me get over melancholy feelings." Interestingly, this boy's interpretation of the theme of "Autobiography" is very different from Kan and Hayes' political interpretation of the same song, as cited above. One of the very powerful features of rock music, especially heavy metal music, is the open horizon of meaning for its songs. The intensive use of metaphoric imagery allows audience members to interpret the song and apply the feelings of the music to the personal needs of their everyday lives. In the movement towards capitalism, these personal needs supplant political needs. In this respect, Polish teens are becoming more like American teens (Kotarba 2002c).

By the beginning of the twenty-first century, working-class teens' tastes in music have changed much as they have in the West. Interest in heavy metal music in general has been limited to two themes. First, the teenage boys Joe talked with in Katowice still enjoy "death metal" music, a style of heavy metal music spiced with quasi-satanic lyrics and horror movie imagery that was very popular among working-class youth in Poland even before the revolution. Their sources for death metal music, however, reflect the more general globalization of their culture: Scandinavian countries, Western Europe, Eastern Europe as well as the United States. Music television from Germany contains a significant amount of German heavy metal. Second, they voice great interest in "classic" rock, especially 70s hard rock such as Led Zeppelin. This music is available through many sources, including Euro MTV.

Like their counterparts in the West, working-class boys in Poland are most excited about rap music and rock music integrated with rap (e.g., Kid Rock). The meaning of rap music has changed considerably since Joe began this study. In 1992, the kids Joe talked with from all backgrounds were fascinated by rap music, including Ice Cube, Ice T, Public Enemy, and Sister Soulja. The working-class boys were especially drawn to rap because of its sheer volume and power, but also because of its apparent function as a window to ever-intriguing American issues such as race and ethnic relations. They were familiar with the political controversy over the Ice T song, "Cop Killer." They were very anxious to talk about the Rodney King affair in Los Angeles. A common interpretation of the Polish news media coverage of these events was that the United States is racked by racial violence, and that rap music is the distinct voice of politically disenfranchised and militant African-American youth.

In 2000, the working class boys Joe talked with appreciated rap more for its lifestyle dimensions and its compatibility with rock music. They all spoke well of recent Polish attempts at rap music. A universal favorite is Kazic, who was also the lead singer for the most popular band in Poland, KULT. His rap songs talk about very current political issues in Poland. For example, one song repeats the line, "Lech, where are my ten million zloty?" in reference to former President Walesa's unfulfilled campaign promise to give all Polish citizens the equivalent of $667 once he was elected. The respondents downplayed the significance of explicitly sexist lyrics in Kazic's music, such as his "I'm on Fire" (cf. Bollag 1992). Kazic continues to be the single most popular musical performer in Poland.

Boys and girls from the working class showed great interest in a major element of social class cultural conflict in Poland: "disco polo." Disco polo is a very simple if not primitive form of disco music unique to the Polish media. There are television programs in Poland devoted to hours of broadcasting disco polo videos. To an American observer, disco polo music videos come across as almost a parody of American youth culture. The lyrics are almost childlike, but contain a bit of sexual overtone. The music videos are basically about having fun. They typically involve groups of young people either partying at the beach, riding around in convertibles, dancing at discos. The working-class kids Joe talked to noted the globalization function of disco polo. For example, a 19-year-old girl who regularly patronizes a popular disco in Cracow with her friends noted: "I like disco polo because it's fun. We like to dance and disco polo is fun to dance to. . . . The videos show us how young people in America have fun. They're lucky: lots of beaches to party on. We don't have beaches like that here in Poland." Working-class teens in Poland still depend primarily on radio and television for their music. Television ownership is virtually universal in urban Poland. Although most of the kids Joe talked to owned boom boxes with CD players, they simply could not afford to purchase CDs. Many observers argued that the underground, "bootlegged" taped music industry in pre-revolution Poland was to a large extent the result of a shortage of licensed, recorded music from the West. The continuing existence of this industry denotes the continuing high cost, of commercial tapes and CDs in Poland.

Middle-Class Teens: Freedom to Taste the Market

In 1992, the middle-class teens Joe talked with preferred what they referred to as "college" rock groups such as R.E.M. and U2. This musical genre, with its thoughtful lyrics and modest stage persona, was conducive to their concern for broad, economic and political issues such as environmental protection and European solidarity. (The three most popular prospective university majors among this group, incidentally, were environmental science, business and English.)

The middle-class kids Joe talked to were also drawn to sophisticated forms of hard rock, such as grunge or alternative bands such as Nirvana and Soundgarden that were very popular in the early 1990s. Furthermore, interest in these musical styles was a passion for the culturally critical intelligentsia in Poland, emerging as a cultural bridge across generations as well as social classes. He met a middle-aged woman at a party on his last evening in Wroclaw, a teacher and scholar in existential philosophy at the university. He had heard earlier in his visit that she was a fan of heavy metal music, someone with whom Joe needed to talk. In preparation for his trip to Poland, he was told to bring precious rock music tapes to distribute as "good guest" gifts. He gave his last good guest gift to her, a Faith No More tape. She loved the tape, and she told him that she shared her love for heavy metal and grunge with her 17-year-old son. When Joe told her that this kind of mother–son bond is unusual in the United States, she was dismayed. She noted that elements of Western culture are so intriguing and valuable in Poland that there is no need to invoke unnecessary criteria of taste, just to make a parental point.

There is one other interpretation of the inter-generational desire for Western popular music. This mother is part of a generation who grew up under the totalitarian control of culture by the communist regime. Although the Voice of America broadcast rock and roll music to the Communist Bloc beginning in the 1950s, Polish people could only listen to these broadcasts in secret (see Pells 1997). As a university student, the woman likely experienced government produced propaganda radio piped into her dormitory room (Dziegiel 1998: 146). Free access to Western popular music of any style was likely as liberating for her as for her son.

The musical tastes and experiences of middle-class teens since 2000 have become perhaps even more complex and fragmented than those of working-class teens. Middle-class girls show great interest in feminist music and musical themes, for example, Bonnie Raitt's and Annie Lennox' work. But, they also enjoy romantic teen music such as Justin Timberlake. At the same time, middle-class teens enjoy the renaissance in Polish popular music. Polish folk music, especially from the Tatra Mountains area, is very popular in recordings and in concert. An extremely popular act is the duo Kayah and Bregovic. They sing pretty, folk-like songs derived from both Polish and Baltic culture.

Social class differences linger strongly in terms of the disco polo phenomenon discussed above. A first-year, female university student in Cracow voiced her disdain for the genre: "Disco polo is just stupid. The music all sounds the same. The people in the videos acts like fools. They dress like they found clothes from the 1970s in the rubbish. Only people in the country, the peasants could like this ugh, kind of thing." Both males and females indicate great enthusiasm for the trend in Polish rock music to highlight America and American culture through lyrics. One hard rock band, Quo Vadis, recorded an extremely popular song in 1993 called: "Ameryka." This song largely celebrates America by exclaiming its many great accomplishments over a short—by European standards—200-year history. The song states that America is a symbol of freedom for the rest of the admiring world.

Discussion

These findings from ethnographic conversations and observations suggest that taste and experience with popular music among teenagers in Poland is evolving in terms of several trends. Although virtually all teenagers Joe talked to have access to radio and television, social class differences remain and evolve in a particularly Polish way. The dispute over disco polo closely resembles the traditional animosity between the urban middle class, who self-identify as "intelligentsia," and the rural working-class peasantry.

Yet, young people from all backgrounds voiced familiarity with heavy metal music from Germany, techno dance music from Denmark, hard rock form Italy, and death metal from the Baltic. Although they are not limited to American music as their primary source of Western teen culture, they still desire and admire American popular culture in general. In a recent *New York Times* (1994: 31) article, a list of the most popular American movies, television programs, and pop musical artists was compiled. The most popular American musical artists in Poland were Whitney Houston, Aerosmith, R.E.M., and Guns 'n' Roses—representing a fairly diverse group of styles.

Teenagers no longer have to travel to Berlin or Warsaw to purchase the latest CDs, but they must have the money to do so in their own cities. The great equalizer may turn out to be the Internet. Computers are widely available in Poland, both in schools and in the home. Like Sony televisions and VCRs, they are generally quite affordable. As Internet connections become affordable (and free, as is the trend in the U.S.), young people gain tremendous access to all the music available through services like MP3 and rollingstone.com.

The major finding of this study has been the convergence of Polish and American views on what it means culturally to be young. This convergence can be summarized in terms of the concept of "teenager." Sociologically, "teenager" does not refer to a person, but to a status or a social identity. Hine (1999) describes the history and complexity of this idea in great detail. Although the movement towards conceptualizing young people as adolescents and warehousing them in high schools can be traced at least as far back as the Great Depression, the term "teenager" gained currency after World War II. The term "teenager" refers to the period in life between childhood and adulthood marked by high levels of leisure time consumption (Frith 1981). Widespread affluence following World War II enabled middle-class and working-class families to survive on the parents' income, freeing adolescents from economic responsibilities. Adolescents populated high schools during the day and spent their allowances on cars, movies, and records at night. Young people had the opportunity to give much of their time and attention to dating, fun, and other youthful concerns. The marketing of music to teenagers addressed these concerns with Top 40 radio, 45 r.p.m. records, sock hops, and fan clubs. Political issues were not of much concern to teenagers until the next decade.

Young people in Poland experience a similar cultural process. As the capitalistic revolution gains momentum, and as a market economy takes hold, we would expect more young people to experience increasing leisure time. An identity based upon consumption and fun is replacing one based upon the political need to account for an oppressive government and the lack of available work.

Young people in Poland, however, are not likely to recreate and relive the naïve world of 1950s American youth. American youth have evolved way beyond the teenage golden age of the 1950s and 1960s, with its Archie comic books, 45 records, and bobbysoxers. As Hine notes (1999: 82):

> This generation [of American teenagers] has grown up in a period of declining personal income and increasing inequality. A sizable percentage consists of the children of immigrants. Educational aspirations are very high, and no wonder: You need a college education today to make a salary equivalent to that of a high school graduate in 1970.

To the degree Hine's assessment of American youth is correct, then Polish youth are not in fact that far behind. Joe's respondents in Poland form all background voiced collective concern that the revolution of 1989 did not solve all their problems, and probably created some new ones. They are concerned that well-paying jobs may not be there upon graduation from either the prestigious Jagiellonian University or the local trade school. They are increasingly aware of what they share with teenagers in other societies: a complex world that requires limited expectations and practical approaches to life. Their complex experiences of popular music reflect this reality.

ROCK EN *ESPAÑOL*

Several terms have been used to describe rock music sung in Spanish, including Latin rock, rockero, and Spanish rock music. We prefer the term *rock en Español* because it has wide currency in the popular music world, and it emphasizes the critical importance of the Spanish language to the music. We will discuss *rock en Español* through a case study analysis of the scene in Houston, Texas. Houston is emerging as a vibrant performance and recording center, with important artistic and industrial links to the music scenes in San Francisco, California and Monterrey, Mexico.

Adopting members' definitions of styles of or trends in popular music for sociological analysis is risky. Commonsense musical terminology is used for many different artistic and marketing reasons, which are unlikely to coincide with sociological conceptual needs (Lofland and Lofland 1995: 164). A working definition for this study that places it within the literature on the sociology of rock 'n' roll posits *rock en Español as an international movement to create and perform original rock music in Spanish which incorporates themes relevant to the everyday lives of Latino artists and their audiences.* Furthermore, one of the major differences between *rock en Español* and earlier styles of rock music incorporating Spanish or performed by Latino artists is that the former is not simply a translation of the American rock idiom or English rock lyrics into Spanish.

This section presents three sociological observations on *rock en Español.* First, *rock en Español* is important sociologically simply because it is a recent trend in popular music. The sociology of popular music is distinguished for its efforts to monitor developments in the rapidly changing world of popular music, and to discover their relationships to other social processes. For example, the sociology of popular music commented early on the societal discourse on morality, children, and the institution of the family occasioned by 1960s protest music (Flacks 1971) and 1990s rap music (Mitchell 1996).

Second, *rock en Español* illustrates culturally the process by which immigrants are absorbed into American society. We will argue that *rock en Español* is primarily an effort among third generation Latinos to generate a music that integrates their Latino heritage, love for the Spanish language, and awareness of and concern for current Latino political issues into their increasingly assimilated positions in and influence on mainstream American society. The fact that the core group of Latinos constructing *rock en Español* are third-generation Americans explains the concerted effort to create a music in Spanish that contrasts with and is not simply derived from their parents' preferred popular music (e.g., Tejano or Conjunto music).

Third, *rock en Español* provides an analytical window to the process of globalization. *Rock en Español* is an international activity that reflects the way Latino culture increasingly transcends traditional nationalistic, political and historical boundaries. We will argue that the globalization of Latino culture will be a hallmark of the culture of the America's in the next century.

The Scene

John Irwin's (1977) concept of the *scene* is a useful framework for analyzing emerging cultural phenomena like *rock en Español.* The scene is an inclusive concept that includes everyone related to a cultural phenomenon (e.g., artists, audiences, management, vendors and critics); the ecological location of the phenomenon (e.g., districts, clubs, recording studios, and rehearsal rooms); and the products of this interaction (e.g., advertisements, concerts, recordings, and critical reviews). Scenes generally emerge around entertainment-oriented phenomena. People enter or join a scene for its expressive and direct gratification, not future gratification. Participation is voluntary, and access is generally available to the public, occasionally for the simple price of admission. Irwin argues that social scenes proliferated in American society after the conclusion of World War II. Widespread prosperity gave people leisure time and money to engage in expressive entertaining activities. Gregarious humans seek these expressive entertainment activities in crowds, which provide impersonal, particularized modes for interaction. Relationships in scenes are superficial, transitory, and segmental. Participants seek action from their chosen scenes. This action typically includes commingling with others, for example, to make contacts with potential friends, sex partners, etc. Scenes provide physical or sensual stimulation, body motion, sounds, etc. However, scenes also present risks—physical and reputational—to their participants, since the scenes exist in urban locations marked by anonymity among strangers.

John Irwin applied his model to scenes in the San Francisco, California area that were fashionable in the 1970s—such as the Haight-Ashbury hippie scene and the surfer scene. I would argue that his model could be updated for application to more contemporary scenes like *rock en Español*. The concept of the scene is especially relevant to the study of an emerging phenomenon like *rock en Español* because the music *per se* is only one part of the phenomenon. Organizational features of *rock en Español*, such as the "buzz" created around it in the local media and radio broadcasting, are also of sociological interest. The concept of the scene is conducive to comprehensive and inclusive exploratory research on emerging social phenomena, but should be updated. For example, one can no longer assume that scenes are as locally circumscribed as the scenes in northern California in the late 1970s. At the end of the century, the expansion of a scene's economic, cultural and political boundaries through globalization must now be included in any analysis.

Independently of Irwin's work, Barry Shank (1994) described ethnographically the rock 'n' roll scene in Austin, Texas. Shank's goal was to examine the ways a constellation of divergent interests and forces together produced what is commonly perceived as a distinctive and unified music scene. Shank makes two points about the Austin scene very relevant to the present study. First, involvement in the Austin scene not only provided people the opportunity to create a distinctive style of music, but this involvement also allowed them to transform their identities. Second, the music scene in Austin over time came under the powerful artistic and business requirements of the national recording industry. Both of these themes are present in the *rock en Español* scene in Houston, Texas.

A History of the Rock en Español Movement in Houston

Members of the scene in Houston refer to *rock en Español* as *el movimiento* or movement. This term denotes the scene as a growing, fashionable trend that is gaining momentum and popularity among Latinos and others alike. This term does not denote a political movement, although politics in the U.S. and in Mexico are relevant themes in the music. There is a fairly common history of the movement understood by most members. As is the case with most histories, the following account is based upon major actors and events. The major theme in this history is the central role played by entrepreneurs in fashioning the movement.

Like other American cities with Latino populations, there have always been Latino teenagers in Houston who love to play rock 'n' roll. They play whatever style of rock that is fashionable, and sing lyrics in English like all the other bands. An example is Helstar, a speed metal band composed entirely of Latino teenagers from Houston's East Side that was very popular in the 1980s. The common history claims that the first rock band in Houston to actually sing in Spanish was the Basics, in 1989. This account is probably an oversimplification, however. Like other local Latino bands, the Basics have gone through many permutations over the years. In the search for audiences, gigs, and the elusive "major label record contract," they have played rock 'n' roll, pop, wedding music, and most Latino musical styles. In 1993, the Basics' vocalist and band leader, Lupe Olivarez, was chosen to serve as the stage manager for the Houston International Festival. The theme that year was a tribute to Mexico and Mexican culture. Lupe convinced the people booking bands to sign Caifanes and Cafe Tacuba, two internationally renowned rock bands from Mexico. Many Latino musicians in the audience were amazed to see and hear rock bands performing in Spanish. Some of them proceeded to establish a *rock en Español* scene in Houston.

The early leaders of the movement included three local musicians—Ruben Martinez, Salvador "Chava" Toledo, and Alfonso Maya—among others. They individually approached club owners to book bands that played *rock en Español*. The bands that were booked were converts to *rock en Español*, that is, they were Tejano or regular rock bands repackaged. Ruben, Chava, and Alfonso approached Javier Tobon, the owner of a very successful salsa club called Cache. Tobon agreed to let Spanish rock bands play on Sunday nights. Ruben, Chava, and Alfonso soon gained the reputation as the leaders of the movement. They instituted Movimiento Clandestino, a booking agency, and began working as rock DJs in clubs.

Simultaneously, Pedro Rubio worked on the movement through the more formal arts. He helped form La Organización Proctural de la Juventud Latinoamericana, which held events combining rock music with other forms of culture, such as art and poetry. These events attracted the sponsorship of major companies like Continental Airlines and Coca-Cola. Pedro was also instrumental in making *Propaganda* a reality. *Propaganda* is a magazine that combines *rock en Español* with art and poetry. Pedro was also a leader of a local political organization called Comité de Solidaridad con el Pueblo de Mexico. This group added a clearly political dimension to *rock en Español* by organizing the first Festival de Rock en Español de Houston, in 1994 at the University of Houston, in order to raise money for the Zapatistas revolutionaries in Chiapas.

In 1994, *rock en Español* could be heard on radio and television in Houston. Media programming of *rock en Español*, however, has always been problematic and programs have been short-lived. The first programs on *rock en Español* were broadcast on the traditional Spanish language stations, and thus showcased international bands. A number of radio programs have come and gone. A major reason for this high turnover is that the programs are usually broadcast on low-power and low-visibility AM stations at times when few *rock en Español* fans are listening.

Around September 1994, photographer Walter Jimenez entered the scene. When he lived in Mexico City in the early 1980s, he became familiar with the burgeoning rock scene there. When the movement started in Houston, Walter attended concerts as a photographer. He soon began booking Mexican rock bands like Cafe Tacuba and Ansia. He was among the founders of the continuing and fruitful link between the scenes in Houston and Mexico.

1995 and 1996 marked great conflict within the scene. Clubs such as Cache found themselves being strangled by the new city ordinance limiting sound levels in live music venues. Promoters fought over personality differences and jealousies. Club owners soured on *rock en Español* because it was not attracting large crowds like sure-fire styles like salsa could. The inexperience of scene leaders surfaced in February 1995, during a battle of the bands. It was organized by Chuli Diaz and held in the International Ballroom, a huge, hot and sweaty tomb that was formerly a discount furniture store. There were eight existing *rock en Español* bands in Houston at the time: Aura Mistica, the Basics, Desgracia de Inez, Desorden, Flies in Paradise, Insurgentes, Seres Ocultos, and Uno Más. They all performed at the competition, except for The Basics. The audience was supposed to decide on the winner, but things fell apart when an Anglo band closed the show and a very upset crowd dispersed.

Promoters of the scene have had mixed success in getting their bands' records and CDs in retail stores. Blockbuster Music stores have Latin music sections, but many different styles of Latin music are represented there. There are three Discotecas "Musiofertas" in Houston (at Gulfgate Mall, North Freeway, and on Canal Street). This outlet sells Spanish music and maintains a rock section, but some of the CDs in that category are really pop. Discotecas y Novedades Memo in the barrio Magnolia operates the same way. At other outlets, such as the large Fiesta stores chain, *rock en Español* sells very poorly in contrast to the more widely known and highly esteemed *Tejano* and *Norteno* styles.

In spite of all these difficulties, the *rock en Español* scene is prospering. The scene received a great promotional boost in January, 1998, when Tribu de Ixchel was nominated for a Grammy Award (Chavez 1998). Their album, "Entre Mundos" ("In Between Worlds"), was nominated for the Best Latin Rock/Alternative Performance category. The nomination was greeted with great praise in the local music press. A party celebrating the nomination was soon held at a local club, where all the major figures in the local scene gathered.

Rock en Español as a Feature of Postmodernization

Sociologically, there are several discernible features of the *rock en Español* movement that mark it as a break with rock 'n' roll's past and as a contributor to the process as the postmodernization of rock 'n' roll discussed above (Kotarba 2002). I will now examine specific features of *rock en Español* in light of the degree to which these features mark continuity or change.

- *Rock en Español indexes the globalization of rock 'n' roll. Rock en Español* emerged in Mexico, Central America, South America, and Spain at the same time it emerged in the U.S. *Rock en Español* songs are not merely English rock songs translated to Spanish, as was the case not too long ago when many *rock en Español* bands made a living covering popular rock songs for customers in Latin clubs; instead they are authentic hybrids.

Furthermore, *rock en Español* is not merely the marketing of novelty rock songs sung in Spanish, but played in terms of stereotypic Mexican charts, as was clearly the case with Richie Valens' "La Bamba in the 1950." And, unlike Richie Valens, who felt it strategic if not necessary to shorten his surname from "Valenzuella," *rockeros* feel no need either to disguise their ethnicity, or to demean it to make it acceptable to a hegemonic Anglo audience. Instead, *rockeros* celebrate their ethnicity.

There are both economic and cultural factors that help explain the globalization of *rock en Español.* The economies in Latin countries expand because of their abilities to create new markets, such as markets for cultural products like rock 'n' roll; while these expanding economies simultaneously create expendable income for consumers to use on such cultural products as rock 'n' roll. Rock 'n' roll, which Americans have exported to secondary and tertiary economies since the 1950s, is exported back to the U.S. in forms that are distinctively Latin. For example, Monterey is generally perceived as the center of the rock music industry in Mexico. Rock groups that record there increasingly tour the U.S. on the basis of CDs that are enormously popular among their audiences in the U.S., such as Cafe Tabuca and Los Fabulosos Cadillacs. In terms of cultural factors, *rock en Español* indexes the growing cultural pride in and identification with Latin identity. Evidence for this trend in America is the apparent demise of strongly distinctive, local, and previously politically functional self-identifiers such as *Chicano;* and the increasingly pervasive use of non-local self-identifiers such as *Latino.* These globalization processes are also present in Eastern Europe rock scenes, especially those in Poland, since massive change in their economies since the late 1980s (Kotarba 1998).

- *Rock en Español indexes an increasingly fragmented rock 'n' roll audience.* The audiences for rock 'n' roll in general are increasingly diverse (Barnes 1988). The rock 'n' roll industry has contributed to this fragmentation by targeting specific audiences with appropriate products, for example, soft rock for middle-aged woman, heavy metal rock for younger adolescent boys, chic rock for adolescent girls, and alternative rock for older adolescent and college-age boys. Differentiating rock audiences by ethnicity is a recent phenomenon. AlterLatino is Warner Bros.' Latin rock department. It was created about four years ago to promote Latin rock music not being played regularly on salsa, tropical or Tejano radio stations (Chavez 1998). By locating *rock en Español* under the rubric of alternative rock, record companies also want to sell their product to the more general, older, college-oriented, and sophisticated rock music audience.

The audience for *rock en Español* in the Houston scene is interesting because it is not a traditional rock 'n' roll audience. For the sake of analysis in the spirit of Alfred Schutz (1967), we are suggesting the following composite, humonculean model of the audience. *Rock en Español* fans are generally young adults (in their twenties), and either in college or working at productive jobs. They are overwhelmingly third-generation Mexican-Americans who are competently bilingual. They are upwardly mobile in their careers. There are two visible types of first-generation Americans in the audience. The first group is young, monolingual, working-class men (late teens and early twenties) who are recent to the U.S. They can be seen at venues on the West Side of Houston that ordinarily present Tejano or modern Spanish dance music. They attend the occasional *rock en Español* concert for the primary purpose of meeting women. (Though it appears that *rock en Español* events are not fruitful occasions for meeting women, since they simply do not attract the large numbers of young women dance clubs do.) The second group is middle-class men and women from Central and South American countries, who attend *rock en Español* concerts at which internationally famous artists are performing. This group was very visible at the Maria Fatal concert at the Cache Club.

At this point the question can be raised: where are the typical teenage Latino rock 'n' roll fans, the kids who have been notorious fans of heavy metal music over the years? There are at least two reasons why they are not very visible at the venues presenting *rock en Español*. First, many of them are too young to get into clubs. Very few of the clubs presenting *rock en Español* are all-ages clubs, largely because of the high alcohol sales club owners would have to forfeit. Second, Latino teenagers apparently share the same taste culture (Gans 1974) as Anglo, African-American and Asian-American kids do: rap. Rap is the great ethnic equalizer in American society, having largely replaced heavy metal music as the voice of youth (Baker 1993).

Like all rock 'n' roll fans, *rock en Español* fans have developed ways of typing each other. These types allow members to locate others similar to them in musical tastes, interactional styles, etc. *Fresa* ("strawberries") are sophisticated fans, largely female, who prefer the lighter/pop versions of *rock en Español*. They like large crowds and lots of dancing. They can be seen, for example, at the concerts promoted by Edmundo Perez and Vibraciones Alteradas, which attract the widest range of *rock en Español* audiences. *Grenudos* ("nappy hairs") are working-class fans, largely male, who prefer loud, hard rock versions of *rock en Español*. They can be seen, for example, at concerts promoted by Walter Jimenez and Conexion Clandestina, which are usually held at smaller venues with small crowds of die-hard, hard rock fans. Social class distinctions readily melt away at concerts at which internationally-known artists like Maria Fatal perform.

- *Rock en Español indexes Spanish as a preferred language for rock 'n' roll discourse.* When attending a *rock en Español* performance, an Anglo observer is immediately struck by the central place the Spanish language holds in the setting. The performers speak fluent and elegant Spanish, at a time in American history when one would expect young, upwardly mobile Latinos to feel great pressure to become monolingual English speakers. The great importance placed on the Spanish language that typically surfaces in political and educational situations occasioned by adults is dramatically present at leisure-time situations in music venues populated by young people. Put differently, *rock en Español* fans practice Spanish largely if not simply because they enjoy and feel comfortable speaking Spanish.

  The emphasis on speaking and singing in Spanish is one of the best illustrations of the postmodern turn of *rock en Español*. Among other things, *rock en Español* negates the hegemonic priority placed on English by modernist rock 'n' roll. But, language also serves as a cultural tool for the *rock en Español* scene. Members distinguish bands in terms of whether the band in question plays in English, Spanish, or Spanglish. Spanglish is a members' term that refers to a combination of the two languages that is appreciated by bilingual audience members.

- *The role of women in rock en Español is significant and expanding.* Although there are no female performers at this time, women do hold influential positions in the local scene. One young woman works for a local television station as a marketing manager. She is about to launch the first 'zine (i.e., fan magazine) devoted to *rock en Español*. The magazine will focus on the Houston scene, but will cover stories related to activities in other cities in the U.S. and Mexico. Another young woman has been heavily involved in promoting concerts and managing talent, as well as covering the scene for the major, local weekly newspaper.

- *Politics are fashionable in rock en Español, but largely fashionable politics.* The political themes found in *rock en Español* represent the social class, ethnic self-definitions, and evolving political orientations of the artists and audience members. There is little if any lyrical discourse on personal disadvantage or discrimination. Put simply, the artists and their audiences, who are largely third-generation Americans, feel they are part of American society. With a sense of confidence in their individual and collective welfare as Americans, they focus their attention on political issues in the lives of *other* Latinos. It is very fashionable for *rock en Español* bands to perform songs decrying the plight of undocumented workers, with great empathy, but without any radical political explanation for this problem. Another fashionable issue has been the political insurrection in Chiapas. The Basics regularly perform a song that praises the insurgents for their courage to oppose the powerful Mexican federal government. We must keep in mind that the Basics have never previously displayed a political orientation in their long careers as local rock and rollers. The political issues displayed in *rock en Español* politics are fashionable, but they are easily mixed in with dance songs or traditionally conservative rock 'n' roll songs about personal relationships and love. Whether the experience of fashionable politics is a matter of naive false consciousness among people who are deluded by the system to believing that they are masters of their political, economic, and cultural fate in America is an issue beyond the scope and intent of this chapter. Nevertheless, the question can be raised whether artists engage in discourse on fashionable politics because they are safe topics that put the artists at very little risk of exclusion by the conservative and always market-weary music industry.
- *Rock en Español critiques the modernist distinction between high and common culture.* As noted above, *rock en Español* is being analyzed within the scene as a type of Latino culture, much like the paintings of Nestor Jimenez or the writings of Richard Rodriguez. This legitimization of *rock en Español* represents two developments in culture use in the Latino community.

First, it is a clear illustration of a major tenet of postmodern thought, namely, that the distinction between high and low art is disappearing in culture (Best and Kellner 1997: 135). Second, Latino culture has developed to the point where Latinos can un-self-consciously be open to a very wide array of styles for representing their individual and collective experience.

Discussion

We have presented key findings from an ethnographic study of the *rock en Español* scene in Houston, Texas. The major process describes the cultural and organizational ways this scene provides various ways to become Latino for upwardly mobile, third-generation Latinos at the end of the century. Some observers claim that this movement may in fact mark the limits of assimilation. Americanization, through cultural activities like popular music, has not turned out to be totally satisfying for the children of the children of immigrants. *Rock en Español* has emerged as a way to either maintain or retrieve one's Latin roots and culture as a safeguard against hegemonic Anglo culture.

After taking a close look at the *rock en Español* scene in Houston, Texas, we would argue very differently. *Rock en Español* functions primarily as a way of becoming American. The re-discovery of one's heritage through language, culture, politics, and—perhaps most importantly—by discovering one's ethnic links with others is a pre-ferred style of people of the third generation coming to grips with the world of their parents and grandparents. Third-generation Jews and Eastern Europeans are now experiencing the same longing for Israel, Shetl, klezmer, Poland, Chopin and Catholicism. Paradoxically, the rockeros' rejection of their parents' *Tejano* and *Norteno* music in favor of rock 'n' roll is not a rejection of their parents, but an effort to share their parents' world on terms that fit with being an American. They use *rock en Español* as a way of reaching out to Americans and the greater Latin world from increasingly hopeful and privileged positions in their communities.

CONCLUSION

Throughout this chapter we have examined the phenomenon of globalization from a perspective which puts a premium on the every-day experience of globalization trends and phenomena and globalizing practices, Globalization is not synonymous with standardization, with imperialism, or with the colonization of the globe by the West. Rather, globalization can be better understood as a mixing of the global and the local—a phenomenon known as glocalization—which renews the importance of locality at the expense of sameness and universality while positing the local as the true intersecting node of global flows. Globalization, or if you will glocalization, is thus about transforming cultures which were previously thought of as bound to narrowly defined geographic communities into hybrid networks of ideas, symbols, discourses, and practices. This new global order is one based on disjunctions (Appadurai 1996), and one that "is becoming increasingly decentered—not under the control of any group of nations, and still less of the large corporations" (Giddens 2000: 34).

As our examples and case studies have shown, in the case of popular music globalization manifests itself through the diversity of styles and performances, of localities and international outlooks. This manifestation of global trends calls for new sociological ideas, such as those of authenticity and hybridity, of scenes, and identity. What the study of popular music—perhaps better than any other sociological topic—can contribute to a sociological understanding of globalization is a fresh perspective on the deep interconnections of movements of media cultures, technologies, ideas, finances, and people. Musical scenes, arguably more than anything else, force us to play and listen locally and interact globally. In conclusion, what we have attempted to show is that globalization, as Robertson has remarked, is "a very long, uneven and complicated process" (1992: 10).

BIBLIOGRAPHY

Adorno, Theodor. 1949. *The Philosophy of Modern Music.* New York: Seabury Press.

Adorno, Theodor and Hullot-Kentor, Robert. 2006. *Philosophy of New Music.* Minneapolis, MN: University of Minnesota Press.

Altheide, David. 1979. *Media Logic.* Beverly Hills, CA: Sage.

Appadurai, Arjun. 1996. *Modernity at Large: Cultural Dimensions of Globalization.* Minneapolis, University of Minnesota Press.

Baker, Houston A., Jr. 1993. *Black Studies, Rap and the Academy.* Chicago: University of Chicago Press.

Balliger, Robin. 1999. "Politics." Pp. 54–63 in Bruce Horner and Thomas Swiss (eds.), *Key Terms in Popular Music and Culture.* New York: Blackwell.

Barnes, Ken. 1988. "Top 40 Radio: A Fragment of the Imagination." Pp. 8–50 in Simon Frith (ed.) *Facing the Music.* New York: Pantheon.

Baudrillard, Jean. 1983. *Simulations.* Semiotexte.

Becker, Howard. 1982. *Art Worlds.* Berkeley, CA: University of California Press.

Becker, Howard. 1963. *Outsiders.* New York: Free Press.

Bendix, R. 1977. *Max Weber: An Intellectual Portrait.* London: Methuen.

Benjamin, Walter. 1969. *Illuminations.* New York: Schocken Books.

Bennett, Andy. 2001. *Cultures of Popular Music.* Maidenhead: Open University Press.

Bennett, Andy and Peterson, Richard A. 2004. *Music Scenes.* Nashville, TN: Vanderbilt University Press.

Best, Steven and Douglas Kellner. 1997. *The Postmodern Turn.* New York: The Guilford Press.

Bloom, Allan. 1987. *The Closing of the American Mind.* New York: Simon and Schuster.

Bollag, Brian. 1992. "The Curtain Parts, and Rap Emerges." *The New York Times*, August 23.

Bourdieu, Pierre. 1984. *Distinction: A Social Critique of the Judgment of Taste.* Cambridge, MA: Harvard University Press.

Braunstein, Peter. 1999. "Disco." *American Heritage Magazine.* 50, 7.

Burgess, Ernest W. 1926. "The Family as a Unit of Interacting Personalities." *The Family*, 7: 3–9.

Canclini, Nestor Garcia. 1995. *Hybrid Cultures: Strategies for Entering and Leaving Modernity.* Minneapolis, MN: University of Minnesota Press.

Carey, James W. 1992. *Communication as Culture.* New York: Routledge.

Charmaz, Kathy. 2000. "Grounded Theory: Objectivist and Constructivist Methods." Pp. 509–535 in Norman K. Denzin and Yvonne S. Lincoln (eds.), *Handbook of Qualitative Research.* Thousand Oaks, CA: Sage.

Chavez, Gracie. 1998. "Tribu de Ixchel: Between Worlds, An American Dream." *Public News*, 811 (January 7): 12.

Clair, Jeffrey, David Karp, and William Yoels. 1993. *Experiencing the Life Cycle.* Springfield, IL: Charles Thomas.

Clarke, David. 2003. *The Consumption Reader.* New York: Routledge.

Coleman, James S. 1961. *The Adolescent Society.* Glencoe, IL: The Free Press.

Collin, Matthew. 1997. *Altered State: The Story of Ecstacy Culture and Acid House.* London: Serpent Tail Publishers.

Connell, R.W. 1987. *Masculinities.* Berkeley, CA: University of California Press.

Crosby, David and Carl Gottlieb. 1988. *Long Time Gone.* New York: Doubleday.

Cummings, Sue. 1994. " 'Welcome to the Machine:' The Techno Music Revolution Comes to Your Town." *Rolling Stone*, April 7: 15–16.

Davis, Joanna. 2006. "Growing Up Punk: Negotiating Ageing Identity in a Local Music Scene." *Symbolic Interaction*, 29: 63–69.

DeNora, Tia. 2000. *Music in Everyday Life.* Cambridge: Cambridge University Press.

Denzin, Norman K. 1997. *Interpretive Ethnography.* Thousand Oaks, CA: Sage.

Denzin, Norman K. 1992. *Symbolic Interactionism and Cultural Studies.* Cambridge, MA: Blackwell.

Dewey, John. 1916. *Democracy and Education.* New York: Macmillan.

Douglas, J.D. 1984. "The Emergence, Security, and Growth of the Sense of Self." Pp. 69–99 in Joseph A. Kotarba and Andrea Fontana (eds.), *The Existential Self and Society.* Chicago: The University of Chicago Press.

Durkheim, Emile. 1953. *Sociology and Philosophy.* New York: Free Press.

Dziegiel, Leszek. 1998. *Paradise in a Concrete Cage.* Cracow: Arcana.

Erlmann, V. 1996. "The Aesthetics of the Global Imagination: Reflections on World Music in the 1990s." *Public Culture*, 8: 467–487.

Featherstone, Mike. 1991. "The Body in Consumer Culture." Pp. 170–196 in Mike Featherstone, Mike Hepworth, and Bryan S. Turner (eds.), *The Body: Social Process and Cultural Theory.* Thousand Oaks, CA: Sage.

Fine, Gary A. 1979. "Small Groups and Culture Creation: The Idioculture of Little League Baseball Teams." *American Sociological Review*, 44: 733–745.

Flacks, Richard. 1971. *Youth and Social Change.* Chicago: University of Chicago Press.

Fletcher, Andrew. 1997. *Political Works.* Cambridge: Cambridge University Press.

Foucault, Michel. 1990. *The History of Sexuality: An Introduction.* New York: Vintage.

Frank, Thomas and Matt Weiland. 1997. *Commodify Your Dissent: Salvos from the Baffler.* New York: Norton.

Friedlander, P. 1996. *rock 'n' roll.* Boulder, CO: Westview Press.

Frith, Simon. 2007. *Taking Popular Music Seriously.* Aldershot: Ashgate.

Frith, Simon. 2000. "The Discourse of World Music." Pp. 305–322 in G. Born and D. Hesmondhalgh (eds.), *Western Music and Its Others.* Berkeley, CA: University of California Press.

Frith, Simon. 1991. "Anglo-America and Its Discontents." *Cultural Studies,* 5: 261–273.

Frith, Simon. 1981. *Sound Effects.* New York: Pantheon.

Fuller, Richard and Richard Myers. 1940. "The Natural History of a Social Problem." *American Sociological Review,* 6: 320–329.

Furstenberg, Frank. 2003. "Reflections on the future of the life course." Pp. 661–670 in Jeylan Mortimer and Michael Shanahan (eds.). *Handbook of the Life Course.* New York: Kluwer Academy, Plenum Publishers.

Furstenberg, Frank. 1991. *Divided Families.* Cambridge, MA: Harvard University Press.

Gans, Herbert 1974. *Popular Culture and High Culture.* New York: Basic Books.

Garafolo, Reebee. 2007. *Rockin' Out.* Upper Saddle River, NJ: Pearson.

Garfinkel, Harold. 1967. *Studies in Ethnomethodology.* Englewood Cliffs, NJ: Prentice-Hall.

Gecas, Viktor. 1981. "Contexts of Socialization." Pp. 165–199 in Morris Rosenberg and Ralph H. Turner (eds.), *Social Psychology: Sociological Perspectives.* New York: Basic Books.

George, Nelson. 1998. *Hip Hop America.* New York: Penguin.

Giddens, Anthony. 1991. *Modernity and Self-Identity: Self and Society in Late-Modern Age.* New York: Polity.

Giddens, Anthony. 2000. *Runaway World.* New York: Routledge.

Gilroy, Paul. 1993. *The Black Atlantic: Modernity and Double Consciousness.* Cambridge, MA: Harvard University Press.

Goffman, Erving. 1959. *The Presentation of Self in Everyday Life.* Garden City, NY: Doubleday.

Goffman, Erving. 1963. *Stigma.* Englewood Cliffs, NJ: Prentice-Hall.

Grossberg, Lawrence. 1992. "rock 'n' roll in Search of an Audience." Pp. 152–175 in James Lull (ed.), *Popular Music and Communication.* Newbury Park, CA: Sage.

Grossberg, Lawrence. 1987. "Rock and Roll in Search of an Audience." Pp. 175–197 in James Lull (ed.), *Popular Music and Communication.* Beverly Hills: Sage.

Hannerz, Ulf. 1987. "The World in Creolization." *Africa,* 57: 546–559.

Harvey, David. 1989. *The Condition of Postmodernity*. Cambridge, MA: Blackwell.

Hebdige, Dick. 1979. *Subculture: The Meaning of Style*. New York: Methuen.

Heritage, John. 1984. *Garfinkel and Ethnomethodology*. Cambridge: Polity.

Herman, Andrew, John Sloop, and Thomas Swiss. 1997. *Mapping the Beat: Popular Music and Contemporary Theory*. New York: Blackwell.

Hesmondhalgh, David and Keith Negus. 2002. *Popular Music Studies*. London: Arnold.

Hill, Trent. 1992. "The Enemy Within: Censorship in Rock Music in the 1950s." Pp. 39–71 in Anthony deCurtis (ed.), *Present Tense: Rock & Roll and Culture*. Durham, NC: Duke University Press.

Hine, Thomas, 1999. "The Rise and Decline of the Teenager." *American Heritage*, (September): 71–82.

Hitzler, Ronald. 2002. "Pill Kick: the Pursuit of 'Ecstasy' at Techno-Events." *Journal of Drug Issues*, 32: 459–465.

Hochschild, Arlie. 1983. *The Managed Heart*. Berkeley, CA: University of California Press.

Holstein, James and Jaber Gubrium. 2003. "The Life Course." Pp. 835–856 in Larry Reynolds and Nancy Herman-Kinney (eds.), *Handbook of Symbolic Interactionism*. Walnut Creek, CA: AltaMira.

Hopkins, Jerry and Danny Sugarman. 1980. *No One Here Gets Out Alive*. New York: Warner Books.

Jameson, Frederic. 1991. *Postmodernism: Or, the Cultural Logic of Late Capitalism*. Durham, NC: Duke University Press.

Illouz, Eva. 1997. *Consuming the Romantic Utopia*. Berkeley, CA: University of California Press.

Irwin, John, 1977. *Scenes*. Beverly Hills, CA: Sage.

Jones, LeRoi. 1963. *Blues People*. New York: Morrow.

Kan, Alex and Nick Hayes. 1994. "Big Beat in Poland." Pp. 41–53 in Sabrina Petra Ramet (ed.), *Rocking the State*. Boulder, CO: Westview Press.

Kaplan, E. Ann. 1987. *Rocking Around the Clock: Music Television, Postmodernism and Consumer Culture*. New York: Methuen.

Kerouak, Jack. 1957. *On the Road*. New York: Viking Press.

Kessler, Suzanne and Wendy McKenna. 1978. *Gender: An Ethnomethodological Approach*. New York: Wiley.

Kotarba, Joseph A. 2008. *Growing Old with rock 'n' roll*. Walnut Creek, CA: Left Coast Press.

Kotarba, Joseph A. 2007. "Music as a Feature of the On-line Discussion of Illegal Club Drugs." Pp. 161–179 in Murguia, *et al*. (eds.).

Kotarba, Joseph A. 2002a. "rock 'n' roll Music as a Timepiece." *Symbolic Interaction* 25: 397–404.

Kotarba, Joseph A. 2002b. "Baby Boomer rock 'n' roll Fans and the Becoming of Self." Pp. 103–126 in Joseph A. Kotarba and John M. Johnson (eds.), *Postmodern Existential Sociology*. Walnut Creek, CA: Alta Mira.

Kotarba, Joseph A. 2002c. "Popular Music and Teenagers in Post-Communist Poland. *Studies in Symbolic Interaction,* 25: 233–246.

Kotarba, Joseph A. 1998. "Black Men, Black Voices: The Culture Producer as Performance Ethnographer." *Qualitative Inquiry,* 4, 3: 389–404.

Kotarba, J.A. (1997). "Reading the Male Experience of Rock Music: Four Songs about Women." *Cultural Studies,* 2: 265–277.

Kotarba, Joseph A. 1994a. "The Postmodernization of Rock Music: The Case of Metallica." In Jonathon Epstein (ed.), *Adolescents and Their Music.* New York: Garland.

Kotarba, J.A. 1994b. "The Positive Functions of rock 'n' roll Music. Pp. 155–170 in Joel Best (ed.), *Troubling Children.* New York: Aldine.

Kotarba, Joseph A. 1993. "The Rave Scene in Houston, Texas: An Ethnographic Analysis." Paper presented at the annual meeting of the American Sociological Association, Miami, Florida, August.

Kotarba, Joseph A. 1992. "Conceptualizing Rock Music as a Feature of Children's Culture." Paper presented at the annual meeting of the Society for the Study of Symbolic Interaction, Pittsburgh, Pennsylvania, August.

Kotarba, Joseph A. 1991. "Postmodernism, Ethnography and Culture." *Studies in Symbolic Interaction,* 12: 45–52.

Kotarba, Joseph A. 1987. "Adolescents and rock 'n' roll." *Youth and Society,* 18: 323–325.

Kotarba, Joseph A. 1984. "The Existential Self in Society: A Synthesis." in Joseph A. Kotarba and Andrea Fontana (eds.) *The Existential Self in Society.* Chicago: The University of Chicago Press.

Kotarba, Joseph A. and John M. Johnson (eds.). 2002. *Postmodern Existential Sociology.* Walnut Creek, CA: AltaMira Press.

Krauss, Rosalind. 1991. "Nostalgie de la Boue." *October,* (Spring): 111–120.

Laughey, Dan. 2006. *Music and Youth Culture.* Edinburgh: Edinburgh University Press.

Lenson, David. 1998. "Drugs." *Literature and Psychology,* 4:23–40.

Levine, David. 1991. "Good Business, Bad Messages." *American Health.* May 10: 16.

Lewis, George, 1983. "The Meaning's in the Music." *Theory, Culture and Society,* 3: 133–141.

Light, Alan. 1992. "About a Salary or Reality: Rap's Recurrent Conflict." Pp. 219–234 in Anthony DeCurtis (ed.), *Present Tense: rock 'n' roll and Culture.* Durham, NC: Duke University Press.

Lipsitz, George. 1994. *Dangerous Crossroads.* London: Verso Press.

Lofland, John and Lyn H. Lofland. 1995. *Analyzing Social Settings.* Belmont, CA: Wadsworth.

Lull, James. 1992. *Popular Music and Communication.* Newbury Park, CA: Sage.

Lyman, Stanford and Marvin Scott. 1970. *A Sociology of the Absurd.* New York: Meredith

Market, John. 2001. "Sing a Song of Drug Abuse: Four Decades of Drug Lyrics in Popular Music—From the Sixties Through the Nineties." *Sociological Inquiry* 71: 194–220.

Martin, Linda and Kerry Segrave. 1988. *Anti-Rock: The Opposition to rock 'n' roll.* Hamden, CT: Da Capo.

Matza, David and Gresham Sykes. 1964. *Delinquency and Drift.* New York: Wiley.

McRobbie, A. 1978. "Working Class Girls and the Culture of Femininity." Pp. 34–54 in CCCS Women's Study Group (eds.), *Women Take Issue.* London: Women's Study Group.

Mead, George Herbert. 1934. *Mind, Self, and Society.* Chicago: The University of Chicago Press.

Merleau-Ponty, M. 1962. *Phenomenology of Perception.* London: Routledge and Kegan Paul.

Middleton, Richard. 1990. *Studying Popular Music.* Philadelphia, PA: Open University Press.

Mills, C. Wright. 1959. *The Sociological Imagination.* New York: Oxford University Press.

Mitchell, Tom. 1996. *Popular Music and local Identity.* Leicester: Leicester University Press.

Mills, C. Wright. 1941. "Situated Actions and Vocabularies of Motive." *American Sociological Review,* 5: 904–913.

Mogelonsky, Marcia. 1996. "The Rocky Road to Adulthood." *American Demographics* 18 (May), 26–29.

Moore, Ryan. 2005. "Alternative to What? Subcultural Capital and the Commercialization of a Music Scene." *Deviant Behavior,* 26: 229–252.

Muggleton, David. 2002. *Inside Subculture: The Postmodern Meaning of Style.* London: Berg.

Murguia, Edward, Melissa Tackett-Gibson, and Ann Lessem (eds.). 2007. *Real Drugs in a Virtual World: Drug Discourse and Community Online.* Boston: Lexington Press.

New York Times. 1994. "The Most Popular Lists." p. 31.

Nissenbaum, Stephen. 1997. *The Battle for Christmas.* New York: Vintage.

O'Rourke, P.J. 1988. *Holidays in Hell.* New York: Atlantic Monthly Press.

Pacini-Hernandez, Deborah. 1993. "Spanish Caribbean Perspectives on World Beat." *The World of Music* (Berlin), 35: 48–69.

Pareles, Jon. 1988. "Heavy Metal, Weighty Words." *The New York Times Magazine,* July 10: 26–27.

Parsons, Talcott. 1949. *Essays in Sociological Theory, Pure and Applied.* Glencoe, IL: The Free Press.

Paterson, Mark. 2005. *Consumption and Everyday Life.* New York: Routledge.

Pekacz, Joseph. 1992. "On Some Dilemmas of Polish Post-Communist Rock Music in Eastern Europe." *Popular Music,* 11, 2.

Pells, Richard. 1997. *Not Like Us.* New York: Basic Books.

Peterson, Richard A. 1997. *Creating Country Music: Fabricating Authenticity*. Chicago: The University of Chicago Press.

Riesman, David 1950. *The Lonely Crowd*. New Haven, CT: Yale University Press.

Ritzer, George. 1993. *The McDonaldization of Society*. New York: Pine Forge Press.

Robertson, Roland. 1992. *Globalization: Social Theory and Global Culture*. London: Sage.

Ryback, Timothy W. 1990. *Rock Around the Bloc: A History of Rock Music in Eastern Europe and the Soviet Union*. New York: Oxford University Press.

Sartre, Jean-Paul. 1945. *The Age of Reason*. Paris: Gallimard.

Sasinska-Klas, Teresa (ed.) 1993. *Beyond Solidarnosc: Essays on Poland's Past and Present*. Guelph University Press: Guelph.

Schutz, Alfred. 1967. *Phenomenology of the Social World* (George Walsh and Frederick Lehnert, eds.). Evanston, IL: Northwestern University Press.

Scott, Marvin B. and Stanford Lyman. 1975. "Accounts." Pp. 171–191 in Dennis Brissett and Charles Edgley (eds.), *Life as Theater: A Dramaturgical Sourcebook*. Chicago: Aldine.

Seay, D. and Neely, M. 1986. *Stairway to Heaven*. New York: Ballantine.

Shank, Barry. 1994. *Dissonant Identities: The rock 'n' roll Scene in Austin*. London: Wesleyan University Press.

Shuker, Roy. 2001. *Popular Music: The Key Concepts*. New York: Routledge.

Stahl, Matthew Wheelock. 2004. "A Moment Like This: *American Idol* and Narratives of Meritocracy." Pp. 212–233 in Christopher, Washburne and Maiken Derno (eds.), *Bad Music: The Music We Love to Hate*. New York: Routledge.

Stuessy, J. and Lipscomb, S. 1999. *rock 'n' roll: Its History and Stylistic Development* (3rd edn). Upper Saddle River, NJ: Prentice-Hall.

Turner, Victor. 1975. *Dramas, Fields, and Metaphors*. Ithaca, NY: Cornell University Press.

Ulman, Richard and Harry Paul. 2006. *The Self Psychology of Addiction and Its Treatment*. New York: Brunner-Routledge.

Vannini, Phillip. 2008. "Social Semiotics." Forthcoming in Michael H. Jacobsen (ed.), *Sociology of the Unnoticed: An Introduction to the Sociologies of Everyday Life*. London: Palgrave Macmillan.

Veblen, Thorsten. 2006. *Conspicuous Consumption*. New York: Penguin.

Washburne, Christopher and Maiken Derno (eds.). 1999. *Bad Music: The Music We Love to Hate*. New York: Routledge.

Weber, Max. 1918 (1946). "Politics as a Vocation." Pp. 118–129 in Hans Gerth and C. Wright Mills (eds.), *Essays in Sociology*. Fair Lawn, NJ: Oxford University Press.

Weinstein, Deena. 1991. *Heavy Metal: A Cultural Sociology*. New York: Lexington Books.

West, Candace and Don Zimmerman. 2002. "Doing Gender." Pp. 42–47 in

Stevi Jackson and Sue Scott (eds.), *Gender: A Sociological Reader*. New York: Routledge.

Williams, Wendy M. 1998. "Do Parents Matter?" *Chronicle of Higher Education*, 45 (December 11): B6–B7.

Wilson, Stan Le Roy. 1989. *Mass Media/Mass Culture*. New York: Random House.

Yalom, Irving D. 1980. *Existential Psychotherapy*. New York: Basic Books.

Zurcher, Louis. 1977. *The Mutable Self*. Beverly Hills, CA: Sage.

PERMISSIONS

p. 8, "Hunger Strike" by Christopher J. Cornell. Used by permission of SONY/ATV Music Publishing.

p. 63, "I'll be Your Everything" by Steven R. Durham, Shuki Y Levy, Timothy James Price, Haim Saban, and Joshua Allen Stevens. Used by permission of Alfred Publishing.

p. 80, "The Dead Flag Blues" by Efrim Menuck. Used by permission of Rough-Trade Publishing.

p. 107, "Heart of Innocence" by Gary B. Baker, Paula C. Carpenter, Frank Joseph Myers, and Jessica Ann Simpson. Used by permission of Red Cape Songs and Universal Music.

pp. 107–8, "My Humps" by Will Adams and David Payton. Used by permission of The Royalty Network, Inc. and Hal Leonard Corporation.

INDEX

169